D0219966

Understanding the
Research Process

WITHDRAWN
UTSA Libraries

Understanding the Research Process

Paul Oliver

Los Angeles | London | New Delhi
Singapore | Washington DC

© Paul Oliver 2010

Apart from any fair dealing for the purposes of research
or private study, or criticism or review, as permitted
under the Copyright, Designs and Patents Act, 1988, this
publication may be reproduced, stored or transmitted in
any form, or by any means, only with the prior
permission in writing of the publishers, or in the case
of reprographic reproduction, in accordance with the
terms of licences issued by the Copyright Licensing
Agency. Enquiries concerning reproduction outside
those terms should be sent to the publishers.

SAGE Publications Ltd
1 Oliver's Yard
55 City Road
London EC1Y 1SP

SAGE Publications Inc.
2455 Teller Road
Thousand Oaks, California 91320

SAGE Publications India Pvt Ltd
B 1/I 1 Mohan Cooperative Industrial Area
Mathura Road
New Delhi 110 044

SAGE Publications Asia-Pacific Pte Ltd
33 Pekin Street #02-01
Far East Square
Singapore 048763

Library of Congress Control Number: 2009932918

British Library Cataloguing in Publication data

A catalogue record for this book is available from
the British Library

ISBN 978-1-84920-111-7
ISBN 978-1-84920-112-4 (pbk)

Typeset by C&M Digitals (P) Ltd, Chennai, India
Printed in India at Replika Press Pvt Ltd
Printed on paper from sustainable resources

Library
University of Texas
at San Antonio

Contents

About the author

Paul Oliver is a principal lecturer in the School of Education and Professional Development at the University of Huddersfield. He is currently course leader for the Doctor of Education programme. As such he teaches social science research methods, and supervises doctoral research students. His own doctorate was in the area of religious studies, and he also teaches that subject at first degree and postgraduate levels. He has written books in the areas of philosophy, comparative religion and research methods. A previous book for SAGE was *Writing Your Thesis* (2008, 2nd edn). His books have been translated into seven languages.

Introduction

This book is designed to help you understand the process of social science and educational research, by exploring the nature of the terminology used in research. Most academic subjects have developed a specialist terminology to employ when discussing their ideas and concepts. Very often the majority of that terminology has been developed within the parameters of that subject. In some cases, however, where a subject area is inter-disciplinary or multi-disciplinary, terms are drawn from a range of subject areas. This is true of social science research, which employs terminology from a range of single disciplines such as philosophy, psychology, sociology and mathematics. Where social science research methods are then applied to a discipline such as education, further terms are sometimes introduced from that subject. The same is true where research methods are applied to management studies or social work for example. There are various consequences which derive from this situation.

The first consequence is perhaps that this diversity of terms makes the subject of research methods very interesting and stimulating. The synthesis of ideas and concepts drawn from such a broad area results in a discipline which is very diverse and which can be applied in very many different situations. On the other hand, there are some consequences which can sometimes cause slight difficulties. The integration of terms from a wide range of subject areas can occasionally create confusion for students and researchers. Perhaps even more complicated is a situation where there exist different terms in different disciplines for approximately the same idea. This can be very confusing for students when reading textbooks and journal articles, or listening to lectures. Moreover, it is not always easy to understand exactly how to employ terms. Some concepts may be used to express a degree of certainty about something, whereas other concepts may express the provisional nature of reality. Students and researchers need to acquire linguistic skills to use with different types of research concepts. In addition, whatever the original discipline studied by a student, they need to develop a basic competence in subjects such as sociology and philosophy in order to be able write effectively about social science research methods.

Having outlined the situation, I hope that this book will help you to do some or all of the following. It should help you to use the specialist terminology of social science research in an appropriate context. It should also help you to understand the meaning of research terms, and to distinguish between the appropriate and inappropriate uses of research terminology. Finally, the book should help you in writing lucidly about research topics, and to disseminate your own research in a good academic and scholarly style.

The book tries to achieve this by identifying as many as possible of the key words and terms which are employed in social science research. These are then grouped into thematic areas such as 'the scientific method' or 'questions of ethics'. These themes form the basis of the chapters of the book. At the beginning of each chapter you will find a list of the key terms discussed in that chapter. It is perhaps worth pointing out that it is generally preferable to avoid defining research terms as if we could summarize them in a brief dictionary-style definition. These are usually far too complex to define in such a succinct way. If we try to do so, we will often lose much of the subtlety and nuance of a term. It is far better to look at examples of the way terms are actually used. In this way we can begin to get a feeling for the sense and meaning of a term. To this end, the book cites many examples of journal articles in which you will find practical examples of the use of concepts. I hope that you find this book useful, and that it helps you to make progress with your studies and research.

1

The Idea of Research

Chapter objectives

This chapter will help you to:

- Understand the characteristics of the concept of research.
- Appreciate the diversity of categories into which we can divide research.
- Review the ways in which research is supported by organizations and sponsors.

→ Terms used

The following terms are discussed in this chapter: accumulation; action research; applied research; autobiographical research; basic research; case study research; commissioned research; correlational research; description; evaluation research; explanation; generalization; insider research; life history research; outsider research; policy-linked research; prediction; pure research; research; research tender; social research; sponsored research; theory; understanding; validation; verification.

The characteristics of research

As this book is about **research**, it seems appropriate that we should devote the first chapter to an analysis of the nature of research, and of the ways in which the term is used. 'Research' is not an exclusively academic word. We sometimes employ it in ordinary language, to refer to the collection of information. If we are planning a visit overseas, we might say that we are 'going to research the cheapest flights', for example. Used in this way, the word carries not only the implication of collecting information, but also of collecting that information in a particular way. It suggests for example, that we do not intend to make a quick, random search of all flights, but rather a detailed and systematic investigation of the options available to us. The term 'research' can also be applied in everyday language, to a wide range of contexts and subjects. It is not limited to one or two areas. Thus, in an everyday sense, research is about collecting information in a systematic manner, on a range of topics.

Fortunately perhaps, this term is used in exactly the same sense in academic or scientific enquiry, although it does have one or two additional connotations. In its most basic sense, research involves collecting information on something, and thus adding to our overall knowledge. Such additional information usually concerns an area which is less well understood or documented, and there are many such areas within social science and education. I have a number of friends who all work in different jobs, but I have little detailed knowledge of their working lives. Equally, they probably do not know very much about how I spend my working day. Systematic research could provide descriptions of the working lives of different professions, and so add to our knowledge of the workplace.

However, research goes beyond providing information in order to produce an accurate **description** of a place or social situation. It takes the key features of that description, and tries to understand why these exist. For example, many people would say that stress is a common feature of the workplace today. However, the causes of that stress may be diverse and complex, and may very well be interlinked themselves with many other factors. A researcher would try to take the initial description of the workplace, and then attempt to understand the mechanisms by which stress is produced in some members of the workforce. In other words, the researcher would try to produce an **explanation**. Such explanations may not be perfect, and they may not fit all comparable situations, but they can help us to understand something of the way in which situations arise in society. In a recent study, Tonnelat (2008) investigated the lives of homeless people in a small community on the outskirts of Paris. On one level, he produced a description of their lives, and the makeshift accommodation which they had created for themselves. However, he went further than that, in trying to analyse their relationships with the permanent residents of the area, the police, and the city housing department. He interviewed the people themselves, and got to know them as individuals. In so doing he started to develop an **understanding** of their lives, and an explanation of the factors which affected them. In other words, he began to create a **theory** related to the lives of homeless people living on the margins of a large conurbation.

One of the advantages of research such as this, is that not only does it help us to understand a situation which is happening now, but it also gives us an idea of how a similar situation might develop in the future. So, for example, if unemployment and homelessness increased in the future, and people were forced to live in such circumstances, we would understand something of the circumstances which affected their lives. Research, therefore, enables us not only to understand something of present events, but also to **predict** future events. Moreover, even though this study applied only to one specific community in one large city, it may well be that some aspects of the conclusions would also apply to homeless people living in London or San Francisco. Research as a result provides us with an opportunity to **generalize** our findings and understand other similar situations.

Another feature of research is that it seldom takes place in isolation. One research study can build upon the insights of other research studies. Researchers exist in a community, and share their findings with each other, in order that we can gradually learn more about the world. Research is thus incremental and **accumulative**. More than that, however, researchers do not simply take for granted the conclusions drawn by other researchers. They subject their findings to scrutiny; they examine the rigour of the research methods which they have used; and they analyse carefully the logic by which they have drawn their conclusions. In other words, they will **validate** or **verify** previous research studies or theories.

Categorizing research

Much research is concerned with trying to develop a better understanding of the functioning of the world or of human beings. In such cases the research is less concerned with particular contexts or situations, and more with trying to understand the basic principles which are operating and which will apply in many different situations. This kind of research is often termed **pure** or **basic** research. It usually takes place within a specific subject discipline, and uses a clearly-defined range of concepts. Sometimes pure research is concerned with testing or validating previously-established theories, while on other occasions it will try itself to develop new theories. Within the sphere of education studies for example, pure research usually takes place within one of the disciplines which contributes to educational thought. For instance, pure research might be concerned with adding to our understanding of the cognitive processes which affect memory. Such research within psychology could be useful in many areas of life, but would have a clear application to education and to teaching strategies. If we can understand better the way in which children will memorize facts and principles, then this might affect the manner in which we present curricular materials in the classroom. Pure research therefore will often have implications for professional practice in activities connected with the social sciences, and can also affect the way in which policies are developed both locally and nationally.

On the other hand, some research sets out from the first instance to address a specific issue or problem rather than to add to our knowledge in a general way. Research which is related to a practical situation, perhaps to try to resolve a practical issue, is termed **applied research**. A great deal of educational research is actually applied research, since there is often a great need to resolve pragmatic issues in the process of teaching. Educational managers will want to know how best to innovate in curriculum delivery, and how to provide interesting and informative types of professional development for their staff. Teachers will want to know how to handle difficult and challenging classes, and how to enhance their career potential. Educational policy makers will want to know how best to adapt the curriculum in order to make students more employable. The list could go on and on. Recently Boyd (2008) and a team of colleagues from five different universities in the United States explored the range of teacher training programmes available in New York City. Perhaps interestingly, given the diversity and size of the city, they found a considerable degree of uniformity in the programmes available. They then went on to analyse the ways in which more specialist approaches could be introduced in order to meet specific needs. This is an example of applied research.

Moreover, there is sometimes a clear interaction between pure and applied research. The latter can on occasion shed light on a more fundamental research issue which is widely generalizable, while pure research can suggest ways of addressing practical problems. The distinction between these two broad areas of research, while not always clear-cut, can provide a useful way of thinking about the activity and purposes of research.

A very broad term which is used a great deal in the human sciences is **social research**. This wide-ranging term is used to include all areas of research which are focused upon the human condition, and the ways in which human beings behave and interact with each other. As we shall see in some examples, this could involve investigating the lives of African villagers or the way undergraduates respond to a new approach to medical training. Social research can encompass a wide variety of different subject areas and contexts. For example, it might involve researching the way human beings interact in industrial organizations, in religious communities, in schools or colleges, or in leisure situations or prisons. There is really no situation in which human beings interact which cannot be subjected to social research. Moreover, social research ranges across a number of different academic disciplines besides sociology, which is in a sense its 'parent' discipline. Methods of social research are employed in psychology, social psychology, religious studies, management studies, education and health studies, to name but a few. As social research embraces the disciplines of both sociology and psychology, it interests itself not only in the way people behave in groups, but also in the way in which individuals will think in social situations. For example, a social research study could investigate the way groups of people interact in a religious community, but also the social influences upon individuals in such a situation, and the way these influences affect their individual cognitive processes.

Another interesting feature of social research is that the key methods employed will tend to be the same whether these are used in, say, a school or a large industrial company. While a certain amount of information can be gleaned by observing human behaviour, in order to gain detailed insights into the reasons why people behave in the ways they do, we will usually need either to ask them questions or discuss issues with them. Hence different types of questionnaire or of interview procedure tend to be the most widely-used approach. These methods exist in a number of different variants, depending upon the circumstances, but all involve the researcher trying to peer into the human psyche, and to understand something of the background to human behaviour.

An important feature of social research, and one which to a degree distinguishes it from research in the physical sciences such as physics and chemistry, is that social researchers will spend a good deal of their time reflecting upon the methods that they use. Social research methods are not taken as a 'given' within social research. Researchers are very conscious that their mere presence in a situation can affect the behaviour of their respondents. When a researcher enters a school classroom to observe a lesson, or to talk to some of the students, then the dynamics of the classroom are almost inevitably altered. The students and teacher are conscious that a stranger has entered their social milieu, and that they are being 'watched'. Besides the very fact that a new person has entered the social setting, other variables can affect the social responses. Whether questions are asked in an individual setting, or in a group situation; and whether interviews are conducted in a familiar or strange situation, may have a considerable influence on the research respondents.

 Questions to ask

One of the difficulties for the newcomer to research is the wide range of terminology, and the fact that terms will often seem to overlap. Different writers may use different terms to refer to the same broad idea. For example, 'social research', 'sociological research', and 'social science research' may be used almost synonymously. Why is this? The answer probably lies in the diversity of subject disciplines which are employed in social research.

Within the broad area of applied research, there are a number of different strategies employed. In recent years, one approach which is becoming more widespread is that of **action research**. Whereas traditional research usually gives pre-eminence to the role of the researcher in planning and designing the research process, action research places much more emphasis upon those who are providing the data to become involved in the research process. Action research concentrates on the exploration and resolution of practical problems and issues, either in the workplace or within community settings. It tends to involve the researcher working in partnership with those who would like to see a resolution of the problem in question. Action research is at the same time a more democratic activity, and also significantly more empowering for those who are experiencing the issue or problem.

Action research typically involves a cyclical process of research followed by action in relation to the problem being investigated, followed by more research. The cycle will start with an evaluation of the problem, involving the joint efforts of the researcher and the participants. Typical issues addressed by an action research approach could be a problem with some aspect of production in a factory, difficulties with an aspect of curriculum delivery in a school, or issues concerning the availability of resources within a community. The evaluation is followed by the design of initial data collection, and the subsequent analysis of those data. The researcher and participants will then reflect upon the analysis, and take appropriate action to improve the situation being researched. There is then a phase of reflection upon the outcomes of that action. Next a plan is drawn up for further data collection which, after subsequent analysis, results in further action and later reflection. This logical process may be repeated in principle any number of times, although there are clear practical limitations to extending it too far. At some point there would have to be a joint decision that a reasonable degree of progress had been made in the resolution of an issue. This combination of research with practical action has generated many research studies in recent years.

Nemeroff (2008) used a variant of action research called 'sustained dialogue' in encouraging a group of village leaders in South Africa to plan development strategies for their community. Instead of seeing rural development as a series of goals, the strategy encouraged them to think of development as a process, in which continually discussing, acting and reflecting were arguably more important than a concern with targets at some point in the future.

The interaction between a researcher and a respondent can be particularly significant in situations where data are collected on a one-to-one basis, as is often the case in **life history research**. At first sight, life history studies appear to contravene some of the key principles of social research. They involve, for example, the collection of data from a single individual, or at the very least, a small sample of individuals. This apparently makes it very difficult to formulate general statements which might be applicable in a variety of situations. Life history research attempts to reconstruct significant features of the lives of people, and thus to understand something of the way in which their lives have been affected by the events of the time. It is, however, essentially a different process from the type of research where one collects data from a broad sample of individuals and then seeks to develop a general theory based on those data.

Some social research, particularly survey research or research seeking to collect and analyse numerical data, attempts to be as objective as possible in the research process. There appears to be a danger in life history research of an inherent subjectivity from the beginning. In a close interaction between two people, respondents will clearly select those aspects of their lives which they wish to reveal and discuss, and on the other hand, researchers will also be selective in choosing the elements of that life which they will incorporate in the final research study. This appears to carry the risk of a level of subjectivity which would make it difficult to see a single life in a broader context.

Questions to ask

When we consider the subject matter of 'life history' research, it is reasonably clear what we mean by a 'life' in terms of the existence of a single person. However, the term 'history' is more problematic. It could indicate the principal chronological events of a person's life, such as their education, the main features of their employment history, and their main achievements. On the other hand, the same term could indicate an attempt to evaluate the main events of an individual's life in terms of the key social, economic and political factors operating during their existence. This would be a much more complex task. Important questions for this approach thus become:

How are we intending to define 'history' within this research approach?
What are the key aims of life history research?
When we write a life history, what kind of account will we produce?

The lives of some individuals will be more intrinsically interesting that those of others. This might be because they are important people who have been participants in major events. However, the real interest of an individual's life lies not in whether they have been apparently significant people, but in the manner in which they have interacted with the social influences of the day. For example, the life of a school teacher may not, on the face of it, appear to be particularly interesting, but by considering the evolution of social issues in society, that life becomes more interesting. In the 1960s it was still relatively common to find corporal punishment, including the use of the cane, in English schools. This was generally accepted by parents, teachers and pupils as an acceptable situation. In the intervening forty to fifty years however, this situation has gradually changed. Whereas society may still expect teachers to keep order in schools, and to discipline pupils, teachers are expected to achieve this in ways other than physical punishment. This change is but one feature of many such changes in society during this period. Schools reflect the changing nature of society, and the lives of teachers will change accordingly.

The impact of the widespread use of computers and access to the internet has had a dramatic effect on the working lives of many people. Large numbers of people now have access to a range of knowledge which prior to the advent of the internet was not readily available. A consequence of this is that members of the public are able to challenge the knowledge, expertise and judgement of professionals in a way which was previously impossible. When we go to see our doctor for example, we can prepare for the visit by consulting a range of internet medical advice centres. The internet has thus resulted in what we might term the democratization of knowledge.

Points to consider

In a democracy everyone has, in principle, an influence on and access to political power. In a postmodern society people will have access to knowledge, including that resulting from research. This is empowering in that individuals can access research findings directly, rather than asking for them to be interpreted by others.

The localization of specialist knowledge with a few professionals in various fields has been partially replaced by the general availability of such knowledge. Inevitably this has lead to something of a challenge to professionals, who must now learn to relate to a much better informed client group. This is of course, only one way in which the advent of computers has transformed working and social life. However, when conducting life history research it is interesting to relate life course events to the types of social and technological transformation brought about by computerization. In this way, we can see a single life set within the context of various changes in society.

Finally, it is also interesting to explore life histories in terms of the changes in value systems which occur in society. The Second World War had an enormous effect on European society. People of all social classes, cultures and countries mixed together in a way which had not tended to happen previously. In the immediate post-war period as a result, there was a reluctance to return to the previous, rather rigidly-defined social order, and the consequence was a much freer, less formal society, which evolved ultimately into the liberalization of the 1960s. People who lived through some of these changes experienced a considerable social transition, and it would be interesting to examine the changes in their lives on a micro level together with the broader transformation of society.

Life history research can use a variety of data including, for example, documents, but the primary method remains the in-depth interview. The advantage of the interview is that it enables a researcher to examine the nuances of the life being discussed, and to explore connections with the kind of broader societal changes mentioned above. Some researchers have used other methods, including encouraging respondents to write an account of their life. Such autobiographical accounts do not provide an opportunity for the kind of interaction available within interview research, but have perhaps the advantage of allowing the respondent to produce a more thoughtful and considered reflection. May (2008) collected written accounts from mothers who were either lone parents or contemplating divorce. She argued that in an interview situation respondents are able to present a broader range of views about ethically-complex issues because they have the opportunity to comment on, revise and present the subtleties of differ-ent viewpoints. On the other hand, in producing written accounts, there may be a tendency for respondents to adhere to views which reflect accepted social norms, as they are aware that they will not have the oppor-tunity to amend or discuss their accounts. It is possible to use the term 'autobiographical research' to describe the approach of using personal accounts separately analysed by a researcher. Sometimes, it is possible for researchers to write an autobiographical account and to analyse the account themselves, although this poses considerable problems in terms of assuring methodological rigour.

Among the large number of research studies involving autobiography, could be mentioned Delorme et al. (2003), who studied accounts by young people of when they started smoking, and Furman et al. (2007), who explored the use of poems as autobiographical data. In addition, Leskelä-Kärki (2008) evaluated the ways in which different types of written mate-rial, including fictional and autobiographical materials, could in principle be analysed.

The use of very small samples in life history research provides a connection with the broad area of **case study research**. In some ways this is both an easy and a difficult area of research to define. It is quite literally a research study of an individual case of something, an individual instance or example. The cases researched might be as varied as a single person, a classroom, an organization, a small community or social group, a town, or a hospital ward. Whatever is selected the case will usually be definable by precise geographi-cal, physical or social boundaries, so that there is relatively little doubt as to what or who is part of the case, and what is excluded. Case studies can be very small, consisting of just one or two people for example, or could consist of a relatively large social grouping. Such variation can lead to some areas of potential confusion.

Points to consider

All social science research will have to select a topic for study. Whether a large scale survey is envisaged, or whether the sample for the research is very small, all research studies must inevitably focus upon a particular subject or issue or topic. One might say that the research has to focus upon a case as the object of the study. In other words, it is at least arguable that case study research is simply a different way of describing research which focuses upon a particular topic. One might, for example, plan a case study of an individual school classroom, while another researcher may plan an ethnographic study of a school classroom. It is interesting to reflect on whether these two are intrinsically different.

Perhaps one way of resolving the issue is to consider the types of data collection methods used. Within case study research one can normally use any method of data collection or analysis which is appropriate to the case being studied. It is normally less likely that such methods would include a statistical approach, but this is still perfectly possible. Other research approaches, however, would tend to specialize in terms of data collection and analysis. One could use this as a way of resolving the above issue to some extent.

Larger case studies may also sometimes be regarded as being composed of a number of small studies. A researcher may be investigating a single school as an example of a major case study, while at the same time being interested in, say, the functioning of the senior management team and the social interactions of the staffroom as two separate smaller case studies. It is worth noting here also that the term 'case study' can refer both to the overall research approach and also to the finished product or account of such a study. Thus one might logically speak of either 'doing' a case study, or 'reading' a case study.

Sometimes a case study will be conducted by an external researcher who, prior to the research, was unfamiliar with the specific social situation of the case. On the other hand, case study research may be conducted by a researcher who is, de facto, a member of the case study context and has a social role within that group. Both types of approach have their advantages and disadvantages. In the former category, one might be a professional university researcher who obtains permission, or who is asked, to conduct research into an individual high school and the level of parental involvement within it. Alternatively, the researcher might be a teacher within the school who is researching parental involvement as the subject matter for a research thesis. This distinction highlights two broad categories of research which are often known as **outsider research** and **insider research**.

Outsider research is representative generally of a traditional research model, of the researcher acting externally to the research context, and looking in at it, in an objective and scientific way. Such research tends to assume that it is possible to measure phenomena in a relatively clear and precise manner, and that the researcher can remain to some extent detached and removed from the research context. An outsider researcher may of course gradually become more involved in the research context, and develop a relationship with the respondents. This can happen in various forms of case study research. One of the traditional difficulties of outsider researchers is that they are not generally aware of the subtleties of the research environment which they are investigating. They may not appreciate some of the relationships between respondents, and hence may remain unaware of many of the nuances of the subject they are researching. On the positive side, they can to some extent stand back from the research and explore issues in a dispassionate and balanced manner.

The advantages and disadvantages of insider research are to a large extent the opposite of outsider research. The insider will tend to be familiar with the research field already, which often makes it considerably easier to select a sample for the research. As insiders will normally appreciate many of the subtleties of the research field, they can often collect richer data than the external researcher. They may be aware of various elements of the research field, and hence will be able to take advantage of this knowledge in order to pursue the research aims. There are, however, disadvantages to being an insider researcher. Familiarity with the field means that it is sometimes easy to overlook aspects of the data which an outsider would have acknowledged. This very familiarity with the surroundings also tends to encourage researchers to take things for granted in terms of observation.

It is also worth noting that the two dimensions of outsider and insider research do not normally exist as mutually exclusive terms. Indeed the two categories do overlap a great deal. For example, any researcher who is operating within a research field for any length of time will inevitably develop an understanding of the research context similar to that of an 'insider'. Similarly, an insider researcher, no matter how familiar they are with the field, will remain something of an outsider, simply by virtue of collecting data about the other people present in that field.

These distinctions between insider and outsider research are brought into sharp focus in those situations where the research field is characterized by extreme social disadvantage and poverty. This was the case with Bahre (2007) and his research into community solidarity within South African townships. This ethnographic research was conducted over a period of three years and the levels of violence operating in the township where he conducted the research clearly gave him cause for concern. He employed a South African research assistant who lived in the township, and for a period of two weeks lived in her home together with her husband and family. However, as a white person he was clearly an outsider in very many ways, and after this initial period he decided to live in his own home outside the township and to commute when the occasion was suitable. His research assistant had a mobile phone to contact him when it was judged safe to enter the township to conduct the ethnographic research.

In this context, the researcher was thus facing an enormous dilemma. The time which he had spent in the township, along with the interpretive help of his research assistant, enabled him to demonstrate some of the features of an insider researcher. However, the continual threat of violence, and his clear differentiation from the community under study, both culturally, racially, economically and in terms of education, created a definite sense of his being an outsider.

Many of the categories of research we have examined in this chapter will traditionally tend to use more qualitative than quantitative data, and it is perhaps true to say that there is a wider variety of terms associated with qualitative research. Often research which uses numerical data is simply described as quantitative research or perhaps statistical research. However there are different variants of quantitative research, sometimes distinguished from each other, because they employ different statistical techniques. One example is **correlational research**.

This type of research explores the relationship between different continuous numerical variables. For example, we might wish to examine a possible relationship between family income and the educational success of children measured by means of examination success rates at age sixteen. We may hypothesize, for example, that wealthier families are able in effect to purchase the kinds of opportunities for their children which will have a positive effect upon their educational performance. However, even if we found that there was a positive correlation between family income and educational performance, this would not prove that increased family income caused a better educational performance. In other words, a positive correlation does not demonstrate a causal connection, and it is very important to reflect this when writing about research findings.

It may be, for example, that parents who earn more will in general have higher levels of education themselves, and will in fact be able to provide more effective advice to their children on how to approach their education and school experience. There is a very wide range of possible explanations here, and much more detailed research would have had to be undertaken to explore which was the most likely causal connection. It is therefore very important that when writing about research we do not exceed the boundaries of what we can reasonably claim from our findings.

The sponsorship of research

Another practical variant of applied research is known as **evaluation research**. As its name implies this approach to research is very much functionally-oriented. The object of evaluation research will usually be a new organizational development or a social project. Those initiating the research will usually wish to have a balanced, objective, and systematic assessment of some aspect of the project. This could involve appraising the way in which it is operating and whether it seems to be successful in its fundamental aims, or it could involve, say, assessing the extent to which the staff teams are functioning as a cohesive whole. Evaluation research can either attempt to assess the on-going effectiveness of a project or assess the way it seems to be progressing, or alternatively, it can form a final assessment of the project once the objectives have been completed.

There is no specific methodology associated with evaluation research. The nature of the evaluation may sometimes require the collection of numerical data and the use of statistical analysis. This may be the case where the outcomes of a project are being compared with those of a different project. On the other hand, evaluation research will sometimes require the collection of detailed comments from participants and may also involve the use of interviews or focus groups. The latter was true of an evaluation study conducted by Fjellstrom (2008), in which those involved in a new undergraduate medical programme were interviewed. A variety of factors influenced the development of a new programme of medical training, and one of the purposes of the evaluation was to encourage a process of learning during the evaluation, rather than employing evaluation as a means of assessing the outcomes summatively.

A great deal of social research is **commissioned**; that is, an organization will identify a particular issue or problem which they would like investigating, and will ask a university, private research agency, or perhaps specialist industrial or commercial company, to carry out the research. There are many different arrangements which can be subsumed under the title of 'commissioned research'. The commissioning agency may not envisage paying for the research, but rather working collaboratively with someone on a project or problem. On the other hand, they may wish to support the research work financially, and hence to exercise **sponsorship** of the project. Where a potential sponsor wishes to identify a suitable research agency, then they may open the project to **tender** and invite bids. A variety of factors might then determine the awarding of the project.

A related situation is where a research sponsor is seeking to have some research undertaken in order to inform a possible policy initiative. Such **policy-linked research** does however sometimes raise complex issues. It can happen that the general policy position of a potential research sponsor is a matter of public record and well-known. All the parties concerned will be well aware that certain research findings may be more in tune with the policy position of the sponsor than certain other findings. Although there may be no attempt whatsoever to influence the course of the research, or the interpretation of the findings, nevertheless the research and analysis will take place within an environment that reflects a certain viewpoint. Particularly where the sponsor may be paying for the research, this is not always an easy situation for those involved.

 **Summary**

This chapter has introduced the concept of research, and examined some of the ways in which we use the term. It has demonstrated some of the range of terms which are employed with different types of research. Finally, it has related research to some of the terms employed in the funding and sponsorship of research.

 **Further reading**

Atweh, B. et al. (eds) (1998) *Action Research in Practice*. Abingdon, Oxon: Routledge.

Hammersley, M. (ed.) (2007) *Educational Research and Evidence-based Practice*. London: SAGE.

Johnson, B. and Christensen, L. (2008) *Educational Research* (3rd edn). London: SAGE.

Saunders, L. (ed.) (2007) *Educational Research and Policy-making*. Abingdon, Oxon: Routledge.

Yin, R.K. (2008) *Case Study Research* (4th edn). London: SAGE.

2

The Conceptual Range of a Research Study

Chapter objectives

This chapter will help you to:

- Understand the nature of the terms used to discuss research data.
- Analyse the ways in which we substantiate data.
- Explore the variety of concepts which are typically used in a research study.

→ Terms used

The following terms are discussed in this chapter: analysis; assertion; belief; coherence; concept; conceptual analysis; conjecture; construct; contested; context; data; epistemology; facts; holism; information; knowledge; multi-method; norm; normative; paradigm; parameter; perspective; postulate; proof; proposition; reasoning; synthesis; truth; universal; verification.

The nature of data

In this chapter we will explore some of the ways of writing about the concepts used in a research study. First and foremost, if you are writing about your proposed research you will at some stage need to discuss the kind of data you intend to collect. In everyday language we often tend to use the word **information** when expressing our intent to find out about something. We will speak of getting some information on train times, for example. However, in a research context we seldom use the word to refer to data, probably because it is perceived as being too much a part of everyday speech. And yet it is still used in a very general way when speaking of the background to a study. For example, one might say, 'Prior to the design of the questionnaire, some background information on the research setting was collected.'

One of the commonest errors when writing about data, is to speak about the collection of **facts**. This is inappropriate in most research contexts. The word 'fact' carries connotations of an element of information which is accepted as absolutely true and valid. However, it is part of the general approach to social science research that we do not consider any piece of information with this degree of certainty. Even after a long and detailed research study, a researcher will be very cautious about the certainty expressed when discussing results or conclusions. In educational and social science contexts, research is viewed as an activity which can give us provisional ideas about the world but with no sense of finality. The world is thus seen as evolving and changing, so that what may appear to be true and valid today may be different tomorrow. For these reasons, it is definitely better to avoid using the word 'fact'.

Points to consider

It is sometimes thought acceptable to apply the term 'facts' to statistics. Although statistical data may seem certain, statistics are collected by human beings and will reflect the preconceptions of those collecting them. It is therefore much better to avoid the term 'facts'.

The normal word employed to discuss information collected in a research context is **data**. Before going any further however, there is a small grammatical point which needs to be mentioned. As the word comes directly from the Latin, the singular word is **datum**, while the plural is data. However, in most writing about research, this distinction may appear a little too pedantic for most writers. In any case, it is perhaps difficult to imagine exactly what a datum might be in terms of research. In an interview transcript for example, it might be considered to be a single word or phrase, but that may not be a very meaningful distinction. For all practical purposes then, the plural form is used. It is also worth noting that it seems more common to treat data as a collective noun in terms of agreement with a verb. Hence it is more usual to write, 'Interview data was collected immediately after the staff meeting,' rather than 'Interview data were collected'. However, the latter form is still in use.

One important factor concerning the word data is that it is a completely value-neutral word. In other words, we can speak of valid or invalid data, accurate or inaccurate data, relevant or irrelevant data. Using the term does not in any way imply, anything about the status of the research. It is a word which can be utilized in any research context, whether speaking about statistical research for example, or about interview research.

There is an interesting connection between the term 'data', and the idea of **knowledge**. The two are not at all the same. We may possess data about a phenomenon, without necessarily wishing to claim knowledge of it. For example, we may have distributed a questionnaire to collect data about the criteria used by sixth form students in selecting a university course. However, we may not feel confident in claiming that we have knowledge of the process. Alternatively, we may have collected data on social class, but we may not feel we can analyse the data sufficiently to gain an understanding or knowledge of the phenomenon. The word 'knowledge', rather like the word 'fact', implies a certain finality and completion in the process of trying to understand something. For that reason it is a rather problematic term to use in the social sciences.

Points to consider

Consider the following sentence:
'In this study of pop culture and the spending habits of young people, it is the intention to acquire knowledge of the use of disposable income, and the factors which influence the young.'

The phrase 'acquire knowledge' might be better replaced by 'to develop an understanding of the use of disposable income'. This would be a slightly more limited claim, but perhaps more realistic.

If researchers in the social sciences are perhaps a little nervous about making claims to achieving knowledge in a precise sense, the word is used more generally to discuss the way in which we can come to understand the world. We would certainly want to know more about the world, and some might say that the achievement of knowledge is the prime purpose of research. The difficulty for social scientists is often being able to estimate how certain we are about the validity of the knowledge we acquire.

The validity of data

In relation to this problem, there are a number of concepts which are used in social science research. A **postulate** is a suggested statement about the world which we believe to be accurate. The term does not have a strict technical meaning in research, but is sometimes used as a verb in a sentence such as 'it was postulated that family income was a major variable in this context'. Related terms are **conjecture** and **assertion**, which are used in research writing in much the same way as in everyday language. A further term which is connected to these concepts is **proposition**. This does however have a specialist use, in that it is employed in philosophy to indicate a statement which links two or more concepts. For example, 'God is good', is a proposition linking the concepts 'God' and 'goodness'. The term has thus passed into social science research as a term for any general statement linking ideas.

Concepts such as these are used to express **beliefs** about the world. One of the most important functions of research is to evaluate the evidence for such beliefs, assertions or conjectures, and to judge whether there are sufficient data to **verify** them. Verification is the process whereby we will seek to establish the **truth** or otherwise of a proposition. The concept 'truth' is related to the concept **proof**, and both are problematic in the context of research.

Points to consider

It is not uncommon to find people writing, for example, that 'statistical analysis proves that religious observance is declining in the population'. The term 'prove' is too strong a claim here. Religious observance can be expressed in a variety of ways, including some which might be hidden from a researcher. Hence, to claim definitely and absolutely that it is declining is too sweeping a claim. The same would apply to any claim that 'it is therefore true that religious observance is declining'.

The words 'proof' and 'truth' are generally better avoided in research writing. It is easy to find alternatives such as:

'Evidence suggests that religious observance may be declining'.

The study of knowledge as a separate philosophical question, and the extent to which we are certain about it, is termed **epistemology**. The study of epistemology has been described as 'how we know things and what we can regard as acceptable knowledge in a discipline' (Walliman, 2006: 15). We can also think of epistemology as an evaluation of the basis on which we actually know the things we think we know! Knowledge is sometimes spoken of as being '**contested**'.

Points to consider

In everyday language a contest is a competition or battle between opposing people, and the word has been borrowed by social science to indicate that there exist different views or ideas about a concept. We might say, for example, that 'social class is a contested concept', meaning that there are many different shades of opinion about the nature and origins of class. This might indicate that the concept is difficult to define precisely.

Since the whole basis of how we know something is contested, it is very necessary in research to explain the basis on which you are operating. You will need to explain the assumptions you have chosen to make when stating that you believe you know something. In fact, it is an important skill to be able to recognize terms and concepts which are contested. It is probably a good idea when writing about research to ask these kind of questions about every new concept you use in your writing.

Questions to ask

In terms of potentially contested concepts, these are some questions you could ask yourself:

> Do writers on the subject seem to use the concept or word in different ways?
> Am I confused by the way a writer has explained an idea?
> Are there clearly different definitions of a term?
> Can I think of different ways in which I could employ a concept?

If the answer to some or all of these questions is 'yes', then you are probably dealing with a contested concept!

Once you have realized that you are employing such an idea, you must define it. However, this does not mean that you have to attempt to construct the one perfect definition of a concept. What it does mean, however, is that you need to try to analyse clearly in your mind the particular definition you have chosen to use in your research. This will make your research clearer to your readership, because they will understand the limits or **parameters** of your thinking. I have highlighted the word parameter here, not because it has a particularly technical use in research writing, but because it is a useful word to include to indicate the scope or range of something.

The range of concepts

The particular view that we have of knowledge and the way in which we assume knowledge can be established has a number of consequences in social science research. As Clough and Nutbrown (2002: 28) point out, '... the choice of method will itself depend on much earlier, often tacit, decision-making processes about the nature of knowledge itself'. For example, we may be investigating the decision-making processes of young people in relation to marriage. We might wish to explore the factors which will determine whether they will decide on the one hand to live with a partner, or on the other hand to get married. If it is our assumption that the relevant factors are fairly clearly delineated, such as economic factors, or clearly-understood social norms, then we may decide to use a questionnaire to collect data. In this case we would be working on the basis that there are agreed assumptions out there in society about the nature of these factors, and that in a sense, the data are just waiting to be collected. On the other hand, if we decide that the context within which decisions about marriage are taken is very complex, and that the factors concerned are interrelated, difficult to clarify, and subject to continual redefinition among the people concerned, then we may decide that a different form of data collection would be appropriate. In this case, it may be necessary to conduct a series of interviews with participants in order to clarify their views. It is important therefore to reflect carefully at the beginning of a research study on the assumptions you are making about the nature of knowledge. Having done this, the language you use to discuss issues of knowledge and methodology should then reflect those assumptions.

Some time ago Berger and Luckmann (1967) in a well-known book pointed out that knowledge is very often 'socially-constructed'. When we are forming a view about a recent political initiative by the government for example, we may form an initial judgement but we will then often discuss the issue with others. We are exposed to a range of views in the media. Our own ideas about issues will often pass through a process of evolution, and while this is happening we will probably also influence other people. In other words, knowledge about the world is literally being 'constructed' through a process of social interaction. The job of social research then is very often to try to expose the mechanisms by which knowledge is created in this way.

Points to consider

The word **construct** is a useful term in research writing. Just as in everyday language the word indicates the building or creation of something, in academic writing it signifies the creation of an idea or concept. Thus in an educational context, we might write about the curriculum as a social construct. This would suggest that we view the curriculum not as a pre-determined set of subject disciplines but as a combination of subject areas, the composition of which is negotiated between individuals and organizations.

It is interesting to apply these ideas to the full range of **concepts** we use. A concept is a mental representation of something which we use to communicate with others. If I ask someone if I may borrow a chair, we will both know what we are talking about because we share the same concept of 'chair'. If I asked to borrow a three-legged chair, the person would probably look at me strangely, because such an object would not be part of his concept of a chair. It would probably be part of his concept of 'stool'. If I asked to borrow a two-legged chair, I would probably receive very strange looks! One of the reasons we can communicate effectively with each other is because we share the meanings of a range of concepts. We can therefore have meaningful communication.

It has been argued that it is possible to generate knowledge about the world entirely through the process of **reasoning**. This entails thinking and reflecting logically about the world, and deriving understanding about it purely through the use of thought processes. For instance, it might be argued that it is possible to sit down in an armchair and by reasoning alone conclude that it would be impossible to have a two-legged chair. It might also be argued that we do not need to search the world for a two-legged chair which might be hidden away in an obscure corner of someone's home! We have only to think about the idea of a chair, and of its purpose, to realize by reasoning alone that a two-legged chair is a conceptual impossibility. Philosophers have long debated whether reasoning alone can really generate knowledge or whether it is observation that lies at the heart of all knowledge of the world. In research terms, however, we do use the term 'reasoning' to reflect the logical thought processes which are part of the process of understanding and making sense of data.

Some philosophers have suggested that there exist concepts which have a single precise meaning, and which are true for all situations and for all time. Such concepts can be described as **universals**. Plato, for example, thought that there were concepts such as justice and truth that remain valid in all times and in all places. In contemporary social science research, however, we tend to think more of concepts as being socially constructed. A concept such as 'freedom' for example, may be defined by different individuals or societies in very different ways. Two people could probably have a very long debate about the meaning of the concept 'freedom' without ever arriving at a firm conclusion, and a dictionary would not help here.

 ? Questions to ask

When writing about research, it is generally viewed as inappropriate to cite a dictionary definition of a term or concept in order to explain its meaning. Some people will be tempted to do this near the beginning of a dissertation, for example.

Why is it inappropriate to use a dictionary definition for a concept (even if it is a major, highly-respected dictionary)?
What would be the consequences if we only employed dictionary definitions?

As many of the concepts which we employ in research are very complex and contested, it is important to try to clarify them. This is particularly the case near the beginning of a research study, where we need to be very clear about the way in which we are using a term. To take the concept 'freedom' which was mentioned above, we might be conducting a study on the nature of pupil freedom in the classroom, or student freedom in a university. In such research it would be necessary to start with at least a working definition of the term. However, as there are many different ways in which freedom can be understood, we would need to examine the scope of the concept. This would involve a process termed **conceptual analysis**. This process can perhaps be best explained by using an analogy from geography. Imagine a concept occupying a geographical territory. Within that territory will lie a variety of other ideas which are related to freedom, such as 'autonomy' or 'democracy' for example. Outside the borders of the conceptual territory will lie unrelated or even opposed concepts, such as 'autocracy'. The job of conceptual analysis is to identify those ideas which are within those territorial boundaries, and which are embraced within the overall concept of freedom.

When we carry out conceptual analysis we will normally try to think about the ways in which people use concepts. If we can think of actual sentences which include an idea, then the conceptual territory of a term will usually start to become clearer.

> **?** ── **Questions to ask**
>
> If we are trying to clarify the concepts 'education' and 'training' for example, we might think of the sentence, 'I educated him in the method of changing a fuse'. This might not seem the best use of the concept education, and so we might change the sentence to, 'I trained him in the method of changing a fuse'.
>
> In the second sentence, the concept 'train' might seem more appropriate.
>
> What do these two sentences tell us about the relative meanings of the concepts 'education' and 'training'? Think of other sentences using the two concepts, and ask yourself what it reveals about the meaning of the concepts.

The term '**analysis**' is also used very widely in research writing in such phrases as 'data analysis', 'textual analysis', or conversational analysis'. Perhaps unfortunately, however, the word itself is seldom explained. It is used on the apparent assumption that everyone knows what it means. However, as with many other concepts in research, it embraces a range of meanings.

In everyday language, we tend to use the word 'analyse' to describe the process of breaking something down into its constituent parts. For example, if our car will not start, we might say, 'Let us try to analyse the reason for this'. In other words, we are suggesting that we think of all the possible related factors in the car not starting, and then gradually eliminate some of them until we have unearthed the actual reason. In research terms, however, the concept 'analysis' is used to signify a range of processes, all concerned with what we do to data once they have been collected.

Points to consider

Data analysis can include the following processes:

- The grouping together of data into categories.
- The allocation of names to those categories to develop new research concepts.
- The exploration of possible relationships between groups of data.
- The search for possible causes for observed events.
- The comparison of data from different contexts.
- The use of data to test a hypothesis.
- The creation of a new theory.

Based on your reading of research, try to think of other activities which are embraced under the concept of data analysis.

It is interesting perhaps, that such a widely-used term as analysis is not clarified more frequently. It is sometimes the case with language that the most widely-used terms are those which we seldom take time to think about. We just use them in the tacit assumption that they are universally understood. In fact, as we can see from the list of activities above, the term 'analysis' is used for a very wide variety of processes. Indeed you have probably been able to add to that list.

The concept **synthesis** is the opposite of analysis. In everyday language, it tends to indicate a combination of things to form a whole. It is used in science, and particularly in chemistry, to indicate the formation of a more complex molecule from a number of simpler ones. We might speak of the synthesis of a new drug for example. In social science research it tends to be less-frequently used, although some of the processes often described as data analysis might be more accurately described as data synthesis. However, when theoretical ideas are being discussed, the term is sometimes used to speak of a number of ideas being synthesized to construct a theory. In a related context, Voils et al. (2008) examined the degree to which it was feasible to synthesize results from different research studies within the medical sector. They were particularly interested in the combination of qualitative and quantitative data. They examined a number of research studies, some qualitative and some quantitative, and evaluated the extent to which the findings could realistically be synthesized into an overall conclusion.

Within education and the social sciences it is worth remembering that research questions and problems are often very complex, involving the inter-relationship of a number of problematic concepts. The process of analysis is sometimes used to break down a research question into its constituent parts. However, this can sometimes overlook the very complexity of the study of human beings and human interaction. **Holism** is the philosophical theory that we often need to consider an issue in its entirety, rather than as a series of separate entities. In writing it is often used as an adjective, 'holistic' – for example, in the phrase 'adopting a holistic approach'. Alternatively it is employed as an adverb – as in the phrase 'the research was conducted holistically'. A holistic approach to research may involve the use of a range of data collection processes or more than one method of analysis. In other words, a **multi-method** approach would be used, in order to examine the different facets of the question, and the way in which they related to each other. The use of such a range of methods in the same study is a popular strategy in social research.

Bryman (2006), for example, conducted a comprehensive review of over 200 social science research articles which employed a combination of qualitative and quantitative methods. Darbyshire et al. (2005) found the approach very useful in their study of a group of Australian children. This particular article analyses the effectiveness of the multi-method approach. Multi-method approaches were also used by McMurray (2006) in a study of action research to initiate a change process; by Eskelinen and Caswell (2006) in a study of social worker teams and their evaluation of a client; and by Duckett et al. (2008) in a study of school pupil well-being.

Another way of looking at this issue is that one of the criteria often applied when a research report is being evaluated is that of **coherence**. In other words, research is assessed in terms of the extent to which the range of concepts used will fit together into a unified framework, or whether the data collection and analysis procedures constitute a logical whole. In order to achieve such coherence, researchers will often try to conduct their research by using a framework of ideas which links together all the different aspects of their approach. Such a framework of ideas is often referred to as a **perspective**.

Points to consider

In everyday language, the term 'perspective' is used in a variety of ways. In art, it indicates the way a landscape is represented in order to indicate the particular field of view. In discussing a problem in everyday language, we might talk about 'our own particular perspective on it' to indicate the way we would address a problem.

The term has been borrowed for use in research, to indicate a broad and coherent framework of concepts and ways of approaching research. Thus a researcher may write of having adopted a 'perspective of feminist research' or 'an ethnographic perspective' in their work, to indicate the theoretical framework they have used. Thus Mason (2002: 57) writes that 'Conversation analysis is grounded within an ethnomethodological perspective ...'.

The word 'perspective' is very widely used in the social sciences and in research. Often employed in conjunction with 'theoretical', as in the phrase 'the particular theoretical perspective adopted was ....', it has come to indicate the broad framework of concepts within which a research study is conducted.

A term which is sometimes employed as an alternative to perspective is that of **paradigm**. This concept was employed particularly by Kuhn (1996) to indicate a broad conceptual framework within which we can conduct research and analyse issues. For example, we might consider the scientific method, involving the testing of propositions using experiments or quantitative data, as a paradigm. In such a case, when we work within a scientific paradigm, we will be aware of a shared range of assumptions about how research should be carried out, and about how any conclusions should be drawn.

The term has been fairly widely adopted within the social sciences, although in this area it has come to indicate a framework of ideas and methods, rather as a synonym for 'perspective'. Hence it is quite common for writers to claim that they 'have adopted an interpretive paradigm within which to conduct their research'. It is rare that one finds writers defining the terms 'perspective' and 'paradigm', although their usage perhaps indicates a slight difference in the terms. The concept 'paradigm' tends to be used for a broader and more all-encompassing approach (such as 'positivistic paradigm' or 'scientific paradigm'), whereas 'perspective' is employed for an arguably narrower approach more closely linked to a specific method for collecting data. Examples here would be 'action research perspective' or 'case study perspective'.

Concepts can sometimes vary depending upon the particular situation in which they are used. In other words, we could argue that they are sometimes dependent upon the **context**. A concept used in one situation may have different nuances to the same concept used in a different situation. Concepts may also vary at the same time between different cultures or countries, and between different historical periods. Concepts of goodness and morality certainly appear to differ between time and place, while our ideas of beauty and aesthetics have differed at different points in history. **Norms** are the accepted standards of behaviour or belief which have become prevalent within a particular society. There can, for example, be norms of dress, norms of behaviour, norms of morality, and norms associated with conversation and public speaking. Norms develop gradually over time, and are a product of a particular culture or society. Something is **normative** if it helps to create or to sustain norms in society. Thus principles of justice and punishment are normative. These assist in the process of encouraging or discouraging certain forms of behaviour.

When we are studying a particular research context such as a school, we will quickly become aware that certain norms are prevalent which may not be typical of a neighbouring school. Such norms may relate to the behaviour of pupils in the classroom, the way in which teachers interact with each other, or the manner in which pupils move around the school. The factors which will influence such norms are often the subject of research. However, when conducting such research (for example into, say, the concept of pupil behaviour) it is necessary to determine the specific elements of the concept which will be investigated. In the case of pupil behaviour these might include issues such as pupils working together on projects, pupil attitudes towards teachers, or pupil involvement in extra-curricular activities. As always, when writing about research, it is important to use concepts with precision and clarity.

Summary

This chapter has looked at the use of concepts in research, and the way in which we write about the data collected during research. It has examined the need to be circumspect in making claims about acquiring knowledge, and the grounds upon which we may claim to have learned something through the activity of research. The chapter also analysed the way in which our concepts and knowledge of the world are to some extent built up from interactions between people; that is, they are socially-constructed.

 **Further reading**

Carr, W. and Kemmis, S. (1986) *Becoming Critical: Education, Knowledge and Action Research.* Brighton: Falmer.

Gilbert, N. (ed.) (2001) *Researching Social Life* (2nd edn). London: SAGE.

Payne, G. and Payne, J. (2004) *Key Concepts in Social Research.* London: SAGE.

Punch, K.F. (2006) *Developing Effective Research Proposals.* London: SAGE.

Thomas, G. (2007) *Education and Theory: Strangers in Paradigms.* Maidenhead: Open University Press.

3

Introducing Research
Questions and Aims

Chapter objectives

This chapter will help you to:

- Understand the philosophical context to research aims.
- Explore the sociological background to research questions.
- Analyse the methodological framework within which research aims can be set.

→ Terms used

The following terms are discussed in this chapter: *a posteriori*; *a priori*; argument; autonomy; causation; collectivity; consensus; constructionism; deduction; determinism; empiricism; epistemology; explanation; external reality; falsification; free will; functionalism; generalization; grand theory; hypothesis; idealism; induction; meaning; nominalism; objectivity; ontology; organization; prediction; rationalism; realism; reification; socialization; social control; social system; subjectivism; theorizing; validation; variable; world view.

The philosophical context

When planning a research project of any kind, whether it is a piece of sponsored research or a doctoral dissertation, arguably the first important stage is to determine the aims of the research. This might be thought of in terms of research questions to be explored, or specific hypotheses to be tested. Alternatively, it might be considered in terms of general purposes such as aims. The latter could also be written in a more precise way, in terms of rather narrower research objectives. The important issue, however, is for the researcher to have a clear idea of the direction of the research.

The aims then have a significant effect upon the future planning of the research. The manner in which the aims are expressed has consequences for the type of research design selected, and also for the data collection instruments and methods which will be used. For example, if one aim of a research project is to gain a broad impression of a national trend in an area of education, then one would expect to incorporate a type of survey research in the research design. On the other hand, if one of the aims involved exploring the feelings and emotions of individual people, then we would probably wish to develop a research design which involved an interpretive approach to the data analysis.

One of the advantages to having precise aims is that they can act as a framework which will permeate the entire research study, and which can provide a structure around which the research will be constructed. Finally, when it comes to analysing the results and drawing conclusions, one can look back at the aims and review the extent to which these have been met.

In order to meet the established aims of a study, the vast majority of research will involve the collection of data. Whatever the type of data, it will probably be collected ultimately by employing our senses. We may interview someone, and listen to what they say, and tape record the discussion. In other words, we will use our sense of hearing. In research in psychology or in health studies, we might use some form of measuring instrument. We could, for example, be measuring a function of blood circulation, or of memory. In such a case, we would be using our sense of sight to read measuring instruments, perhaps in a laboratory. Data which are collected through the use of our senses, are termed **empirical** data. It does not matter whether the data are in the form of numbers or words, if these are collected through employing our senses, then these are empirical data. Most of the data which we normally employ in research are empirical data.

Moore (2008) conducted a study of the relationship between social class, race and culture among a sample of Black people in the United States. The data largely consisted of interview data. As these were collected by talking to people and listening to what they said, these can be regarded as empirical data. Nevertheless, in the early stages of this research article, there is a detailed discussion of a number of conceptual issues related to the study, and this discussion rests on conceptual rather than empirical matters. It is in effect a precursor to the analysis of the empirical findings.

This does, however, raise an interesting philosophical question. Some philosophers think that all data are inevitably empirical, and that the only way in which we can know anything about the world with any certainty is through our senses. If you hold this view, then you could be described as an **empiricist**, and belonging to the school of thought known as **empiricism**.

There are, at the same time, philosophers who consider that other forms of knowledge are possible. Supposing for example that we are researching the question of whether warfare can ever be justified. An empiricist may feel that one way to investigate this question would be to visit a war zone and collect some data on a war in action. Based on these data, the empiricist would then try to resolve the question. On the other hand, others may feel that such a strategy is simply not necessary. They may consider that we can simply reflect carefully upon the nature of war, and think out our views on whether it can be justified. They may also think that we can do this from first principles, without actually observing warfare.

The empiricist may feel that it is necessary to observe several different types of conflict, in order to determine whether war is justifiable under certain circumstances. Based on the empirical data collected, an empiricist might then wish to advance the argument that warfare is justifiable in order to protect, say, a minority group, or to prevent the invasion of a vulnerable country. On the other hand, a non-empiricist may simply feel on the basis of reflection or logic that warfare is never justified, because of the suffering and death which are entailed. This conclusion is drawn simply from an analysis of the nature of war.

If we claim something to be true, independent of the empirical data and based exclusively upon an analysis of the ideas involved, then this is described as **_a priori_** knowledge. When we claim something to be true based on empirical data, this is known as **_a posteriori_** knowledge. _A priori_ means approximately 'before the fact', while _a posteriori_ means approximately 'after the fact'.

The notion of *a priori* knowledge in research is important in terms of defining those concepts which are central to a research study. It is very important when specifying aims for example, that any concepts which have a key role to play in the research are clearly analysed and defined. In a study of refugees in India, Rolfe (2008) argued that the concept of a refugee who is held by the government of a country has important consequences for the way in which refugees are treated in practical terms. Arguably it is unnecessary to observe or meet many refugees in order to define our understanding of the nature of refugee status. If this were necessary then we would be developing *a posteriori* knowledge. If, on the other hand, it is the view that we do not need empirical data to resolve the question then we are developing *a priori* knowledge.

Generally speaking, it is probably true that most researchers would regard themselves as empiricists, and hence would not concern themselves too much with questions about *a priori* knowledge. However, there are certain categories of knowledge where what the *a priori* does may impact upon research. Moral questions, issues involving theology and God, and also the propositions of mathematics, are sometimes considered to involve *a priori* knowledge. For example, some people may consider the proposition 'advances in health care are a good thing', to be self-evidently true, since to deny it just does not make any sense. In other words, they would argue that it is an *a priori* truth. On the other hand, some people might point to a person who has fallen into a coma and is being kept alive by very sophisticated technology. They could argue that such medical advances are not really, in this case, furthering the quality of human life. They may also suggest this demonstrates that advances in health care are not necessarily an unqualified good thing.

? — **Questions to consider**

When planning a research study it is a good idea to reflect upon issues which are in principle *a priori*, and which might be resolved before the data collection process starts. This could very easily save time, and thus make the research much more precise.

There are a range of related issues in research, which come broadly within the scope of a branch of philosophy known as **ontology**. The latter can be defined as the study of what we assume to exist in the world. On the face of it, this may seem to be a rather strange area of study. Is it not clear, we might ask, that a red deer exists but a unicorn does not exist? Well, this may be reasonably clear to most people, but let us take another example. Do we consider that social class exists? In other words, are there precise and measurable categories out there in the social world, which we term a social class? Can we list the qualities and criteria which characterize each social class, and therefore know exactly to which social class someone belongs? On the other hand, is social class nothing but a general name which describes a broad, often stereotypical impression of what a person is like? When we describe someone as belonging to a social class, are we simply using descriptive language to give someone an approximate idea of what they are like, much as we might say that someone is cheerful, witty or well-read?

If we take the view that social class actually exists as an entity in the world, then this is an example of **realism** or a **realist ontology**, while if we think that social class is simply the name of a broad, descriptive term, then this is an example of **nominalism** or a **nominalist ontology**. Although most research would not specifically address these terms, their consequences can have far-reaching effects in social science research. If as researchers we adopt, implicitly or explicitly, a realist ontology, then we assume that many social phenomena actually exist in real terms. It tends to follow from this that we also assume that these phenomena are measurable. Within such a philosophical position we would probably select data collection methods such as questionnaires, which assume it is possible to collect data in a precise and numerical way. On the other hand, if we assume a nominalist ontology, then we assume that the phenomena are much less precise, and we would probably select data collection methods such as interviews or focus groups.

Rigakos and Law (2009) have investigated the subject of 'risk' and the different ontological perspectives which are possible. Risk is a subject on which there is a growing research literature, at least partly perhaps because contemporary society appears to entail an increasing number of different risks. A realist concept of risk would, for example, assume that 'risk' as a reality actually exists in society – that we can measure it, and investigate it. On the other hand, it is possible to conceptualize risk in a much more general way, in terms of the possibility of an event happening. We can see therefore, that depending upon our ontological framework, we can have quite different ways of viewing the idea of risk.

As ontological questions are closely related to issues of how we decide to collect our research data, they are intimately linked to the basis upon which we think we know something to be true. We can all form judgements about the veracity of the things around us. Suppose we consult a railway timetable and it states that a train will leave Platform 4 at 10.15 am. If we believe that to be valid knowledge, we may get on the train at Platform 4 at 10.10 am in the full expectation that it will depart in five minutes time. Why do we believe that to be true? There are no doubt many reasons, including our previous observation that the train timetable is an accurate symbolic representation of the reality of train movements. We make these kind of decisions about the validity of knowledge many times each day. The study of the grounds upon which we believe something to be true is known as **epistemology**.

Questions regarding the validity of knowledge are clearly very important in research. When we write research aims, we are assuming that what we hope to achieve in the research actually is achievable in terms of knowledge. In other words, we assume it is feasible to find out what we hope to find out. These aims define the parameters of the kind of data we will seek. Finally, we are assuming that an analysis of that data will generate the kind of valid knowledge which we hope to generate. Empirical justifications represent one means of supporting epistemological assertations. Another set of justifications are those embraced under the title of **rationalism**.

Rationalism is an approach to substantiating knowledge based upon the use of reason. The collection of data using our senses, and the application of mental reason and logic, are not necessarily in opposition to one other. We can collect empirical data in research, and then apply logical processes in order to analyse it. Therefore, one can claim to be both an empiricist and a rationalist. However, there are philosophers and researchers who represent different extremes of both schools of thought. One can be, for example, an extreme empiricist – and believe that all knowledge is of necessity derived from sense experience. On the other hand, one can hold the view of the extreme rationalist – that it is only possible to derive knowledge by mental analysis and reason. There are clearly a number of different positions here which occupy the middle ground. Many researchers would take the position that both approaches are required. Of course we can learn from empirical data on their own, but it is only when we start to compare, contrast, synthesize and analyse data that we begin to really understand these. To achieve this we require mental processes, reason and logic.

In some ways extreme rationalism is rather similar to another philosophical approach, that of **idealism**. This is the view that the only things in the world which are truly real are the mind and the thoughts which it contains. In other words, we can be certain of what we are thinking, but when we look out at the material world it is as if we are simply looking at an array of images, reflections and impressions. We cannot, according to the idealists, be really certain of what we are looking at. To some extent, idealism can thus be compared and contrasted with realism, which does see the physical world as consisting of real entities. The French philosopher Descartes was a famous idealist, and in a celebrated assertion he claimed that ultimately the only thing of which he could be certain was that he was thinking! In research terms, idealism leads us down a rather difficult road. We can certainly collect data about the external world, for example observational data, but we cannot be sure that such data genuinely reflect reality. Hence, we must rely upon the interpretation of others to confirm our own impression of the physical world.

The notion that we make sense of the world around us by interpreting what we see is a very important idea in social research. On this model, the world is not made up of completely precise, definite realities, as the realist philosophers would argue, but rather the external world is much more imprecise. Indeed within this view, individual human beings construct their understanding of the world partly from what they see and hear around them, but also from what other individuals tell them about their impressions of the world. In other words, we interpret the world around us, trying to make sense of it, and at the same time compare our impressions and formulations with those of others we talk to. The world around us is thus constructed, and this philosophical approach is known as **constructionism**.

However, it should not be thought that we construct the world around us in one go, and having made up our minds about what we think of events around us we then stop there. In fact, constructionists see this as an evolving process. The process of constructing reality never ends. As soon as we think we have made sense of things, an event happens which causes us to reappraise those things. In some ways, this is a positive process, since we remain open to new ideas and ways of interpreting the world afresh. Some constructionists see this as the way in which culture develops. It can be argued that a culture is, in effect, the sum total of the negotiations undertaken by individual people, and hence the agreements which are reached about the nature of social reality. Similarly some would argue that it is in this way that the organizations of society become what they are. In this perspective, a school for example, is not a predefined entity with a certain set of values and characteristics. It is an organic, evolving organization with an ever-changing existence. The managers, administrators, governors, teachers, parents and students are all in a continuous dialogue, creating and recreating the nature of the school. Thus, according to social constructionists, objects and social organizations in the world do not have a fixed and immutable character but are in a state of flux, a product of the social discourse which takes place within them and around them.

Points to consider

If, however, everything in the social world is in a continual state of change and transition, then we might wonder where this leaves the results of research! When we reach conclusions at the end of a research project we might argue that, according to constructionism, the social setting has already changed and we need to do the research again! This is, however, not necessarily a problem if we accept that research is located in time, and that others will probably replicate our research in due course.

Some researchers would argue that this social process even applies to ways of thinking which we sometimes regard as fixed and precise. Carolan (2008) argues that even the nature of scientific enquiry itself, and the thought-processes which accompany it, are in part a consequence of the social context. In terms of this argument, one might suggest that while the essential logical process of science is predetermined, the problems we select for investigation, the kind of data we choose to collect, and the way we decide to analyse it, are all affected by the discourse between individuals.

? Questions to consider

One of the potential difficulties with social constructionism is that if every-thing is created through intersubjective discourse, then it apparently leaves us with very little certainty in terms of values. Some professionals such as teachers, social workers and health workers might argue that it is important to have firm values on ethical issues, since without these a profession ceases to have coherence.
What do you think about this question?

A further interesting philosophical issue concerning constructionism, is that of **causation**, or the investigation of the factors which might be instrumental in the cause of a social event or situation. If in fact entities in the world are socially constructed, then it appears to follow that separate individuals may look at the social world in a different way. They may interpret events differently. In terms of research then, it becomes rather harder to be clear about the variables which might be operating in a particular situation. Instead of the variables being relatively fixed, they are subject to change through differing interpretations. This may make it considerably more difficult to determine which might be the causal factors in a situation.

Within a realist framework it appears to be easier to identify those factors which might have been the cause of an event. However, the process of identifying such factors might be viewed by some researchers as over-simplifying a situation. Within a constructionist perspective the variables are certainly less precise, but some researchers may feel that this is a more accurate representation of reality.

Points to consider

In everyday language we do use the term 'cause' as if it is usually possible to say exactly why something happened. For example,' the delay was caused by an accident on the motorway'. However, in reality, 'causes' are often very complex and resulting from the combination of a series of events. The social research process attempts to clarify this complexity, rather than treating 'cause' as a simple, unitary factor.

The logical thought processes of research are central to the notion of investigating the subject matter of aims, and of drawing legitimate conclusions. There are two basic procedures in research. One is termed **deduction** or **deductive reasoning**, while the other is termed **induction** or **inductive reasoning**. In the deductive process, a researcher will start with a general theoretical proposition about the world and then collect data with a view to seeing whether individual observations will support or negate the theory. If the data appear to support the theory, then the latter is left unchanged. However, if the observations do not appear to support the theory, then the latter is adapted to incorporate the new observations.

In inductive reasoning, the process will start with the collection of individual observations. The researcher will then seek a pattern in such data, and if one appears to exist, that researcher will construct a general statement or theory which describes, as accurately as possible, the relationship between the observations. Further data are then collected and compared with the theory. If they support the theory the latter is maintained in its existing form, while if they do not support the theory the latter is amended.

Many researchers will state that they intend their research to be balanced, fair and objective. However, it is often unclear exactly what they mean by **objectivity** in research. The term appears to carry the implications that the research is precise and well-constructed, and that the data can be relied upon to be independent of extraneous variables and other influences. Yet many researchers would regard the achievement of such objectivity as unlikely or even impossible. They would argue that even the researcher moving about in the research field unduly interferes with the research with consequences for the resulting data. The concept of objectivism is related to that of realism, in the sense that it tends to assume that social realities are precise and measurable. Objectivism carries the connotation that we can therefore isolate aspects of reality, and separate the variables which affect them. It is also associated with the approaches of the physical sciences, and the related assumptions that precise, quantitative measurement is a possible and desirable aim.

The opposite philosophical viewpoint is that of **subjectivism**. This idea is very much associated with the interpretation of the social world by the individual, and of the attachment of meaning to social events. The notion of subjectivity in social science research places an emphasis upon the interpretive work which has to be carried out by human beings in order to make sense of the world. Events are not viewed as being precise and measurable, but as requiring human intervention in terms of understanding them and then transmitting that meaning to others. The resulting discourse helps to develop a shared understanding between human beings, an understanding which is founded upon a network of subjective meanings.

Some researchers will attempt to be as objective as possible in their research. For example, they might try to avoid writing from a particular viewpoint or perspective when analysing or summarizing their data. Whether to avoid doing this is entirely possible, is a question for debate. Other researchers will be committed to a particular perspective, and will use that to interpret and analyse their data. It is an interesting question whether or not all human beings will approach an issue with some form of predetermined world view. As we grow as children, we are all exposed to different experiences, different learning situations, and different influences. To some considerable extent, these make us what we are. If we are later involved in 'research', then it is reasonable to suppose that we will each look at our data and make sense of them, within the scope of our life experiences. Apple (2008) presents some autobiographical data of his experiences of teaching children from impoverished backgrounds in an under-resourced school. While everyone would no doubt agree that such a lack of resources is undesirable and unacceptable, individual researchers might draw different inferences from such observations. All researchers might agree that the school was under-funded and that there were insufficient employment opportunities in the surrounding community. We might regard these observations as 'objective'. On the other hand, there would no doubt be considerable disagreement about the specific macro economic and political causes of the situation, and about the social remedies necessary. In that sense, the analysis would be 'subjective'.

Linked to the notion of subjectivity in research is that of the capacity of the individual to formulate their own decisions in life. This may concern, for example, the decision to interpret the world in a particular way by selecting a certain perspective such as Marxism or a strictly scientific approach. The exercise of personal judgement in this way is a reflection of our individual **autonomy** or **free will**. By the exercise of this faculty we choose to understand the world around us in a certain way, and not in another. If we are conducting research we can use this approach to try to interpret how others see the world. On the other hand, respondents will also exercise their autonomy. When asked by a researcher for their understanding of an event, they will present that understanding within the confines of a particular perspective. The opposing view to free will is that of **determinism**, the idea that we have very little or no choice in the way in which we attribute meaning. Determinism assumes that another factor or factors will influence us in deciding the way in which we look at the world.

Therefore, when thinking about the purposes of research, there is a wide range of philosophical positions which may be relevant. Nevertheless, in social research, the position of the individual within society is also clearly relevant, and in determining research aims sociological issues play an important role.

The sociological background to research questions

Some social researchers will express their aims in terms of the factors which they envisage as altering society, and hence influencing the world around us in a significant way. Such factors are termed **variables**. A variable might be a factor such as age, gender, social class, educational level, or religious affiliation. To express research aims in terms of variables is to some extent to adopt a realist position. It is to assume that such variables actually exist in a measurable way, and also that the effects they bring about are discrete and measurable. A variable such as 'age' clearly exists in a measurable way, but the same is not quite as certain with a variable such as religious affiliation. We may ask a respondent to a questionnaire to indicate their religious affiliation, and offer them a range of alternatives such as 'Church of England', 'Buddhist', or 'Parsi'. However, the response may simply indicate a cultural affiliation, such that a person had been brought up, say, within the Church of England, but now holds no strong theological or spiritual connection. In fact, when a respondent provides either a positive or negative response to such a question, we will have no idea about the complex range of possible connections with that faith. In other words, as a variable, it may not reflect anything very significant, simply because it is very difficult for us to measure it in a meaningful way. The acceptance that religious affiliation, measured in that way, is a meaningful variable, involves a great many assumptions.

The compromises which have to be made when expressing research aims in terms of variables are thus far-reaching, but in some contexts these can still be useful. Such quantified variables can help in establishing broad trends in society. If, for example, the purpose of a research project is to obtain a country-wide picture of the relationship, if any, between the religious affiliation of a family and the number of children within it, then the use of variables in this way is probably the appropriate strategy.

In order to try to establish such broad trends in society, it is usually necessary to treat phenomena as measurable variables in this way. Inevitably though, this process entails a possible simplification of ideas. The process whereby we consider a potentially very complex issue in society, and then express that as a discrete, social reality is known as **reification**. To reify something is to express it in simple, measurable terms, when really the idea is far more varied and complex. Almost inevitably, reification involves a certain degree of reductionism and simplification. Nevertheless, when we are trying to understand society, and express those ideas in straightforward terms to others, a certain amount of reification is probably necessary. However, we should not lose sight of the purpose of the process and of its limitations.

A major sociological perspective which relies to a certain extent upon the process of reification, is that of **functionalism**. Historically it is associated with the work of the French sociologist, Emile Durkheim. Functionalism draws an analogy between the way in which organs of the body work together to produce an effective organism, which can adapt both to its environment and the different elements of society which, so it is argued, operate as a cohesive whole. In other words, the great institutions of society such as the educational system, legal and judicial system, and systems of government, all function as a cohesive whole. Functionalists would see this perspective as both explanatory, in terms of helping us understand the way in which society works, and normative, in terms of prescribing how society ought to operate effectively.

According to functionalists, individual members of society learn to operate within the institutions of society, and according to the established norms of that society, through a process of **socialization**. According to this view, as we grow up we acquire an appreciation of what society expects of us, and we learn to fulfil these social expectations. At the same time, society exerts an influence upon us to adapt to the prevalent norms, and hence this is an important mechanism for **social control**. Critics of functionalism would argue that we are encouraged to adapt to the prevalent status quo of society, and not to challenge the established institutions or ideas.

Critics of functionalism would thus argue that it is a perspective which concentrates upon stability and equilibrium in society. In so doing, they argue, it does not address many of the inequalities in society, overlooking them in favour of concentrating on their apparent utility in society. Equally critics argue that functionalism does not propose methods for changing society, but again overlooks the need to address inequalities and unfair systems which have evolved. In its defence functionalism does appear to address the process of societal change, but the mechanism does tend to concentrate on a gradual evolution and development of society, which is inevitably a slower process than some people would prefer. Social research within a functionalist perspective does tend to focus upon the role of institutions in society. Such institutions might be individual schools or colleges, or a broader system such as the system of higher education. Alternatively it might explore the overall function of a health service. Research may concentrate on the original purpose of such institutions and the way in which they evolved. It would explore their contribution to the overall society, or examine the way in which they help society to evolve.

Functionalism is thus a perspective which emphasizes **consensus** in society, and the importance of social stability. It stresses the importance of the **collectivity** over the needs of individual people. Thus the fundamental role of the individual in society is to contribute to the overall needs of society, rather than to pursue his or her own goals. As functionalist research is concerned with trends in society, and the way in which institutions work together, it often requires the collection of statistical data. It tends to be associated with data collection strategies which emphasize the existence of **external realities**.

There are, however, social research perspectives that are very different to functionalism, which emphasize the way in which individual people come to understand the social world around them. Instead of concentrating upon society external to the individual, these perspectives focus upon the way in which individuals make sense of the world around them, and thus by their collective efforts at such understanding, create the social world. In other words, such perspectives explore the way in which we, as human beings, generate a sense of **meaning** about the world. When different people view a situation, they will each see it from a unique point of view. They will make sense of that situation in their own terms, and attach their own meaning to it. Social researchers are often very interested in understanding two aspects of this. First of all, they pay attention to the mechanisms of the process whereby people attach meaning to situations, and secondly, they are interested in the nature of the meanings themselves. Rae and Cochrane (2008) conducted a qualitative study of student views about written feedback given to them by tutors. The methodology involved the use of focus groups. Here the researchers particularly wanted to understand the way in which the students looked at the issue, and specifically mention in their article (p. 218) that they were trying to appreciate a sense of meaning from the student viewpoint. In a separate (2008) study, Veltri explored the experiences and contribution made by young teachers who worked for the Teach for America programme. They teach for a time in schools located in more deprived areas, developing their own teaching skills while at the same time making a valuable contribution to society. The researcher noted that the research design involved the use of interview research, and enabled a sense of meaning to be constructed for the young participants in the Teach for America programme (2008: 539).

The concept of meaning is an important element in interpretive sociology, and also in the process whereby the researcher tries to understand the world view of respondents. The use of such an interpretive approach in exploring the social world is particularly associated with the German sociologist Max Weber. However, the task of understanding the view of the world of another human being is clearly not a straightforward one. Neither is it immediately obvious how one would embark on this process. Nevertheless, seeking to understand the meanings which our fellow human beings attribute to existence and the world around us is something which we all try to do, both in an everyday context and also within the more formal confines of the world of research.

	Points to consider

In everyday life we spend a great deal of time in routine conversation trying to explore what others think of the world around them. With this information we test our own views and compare what we think with the ideas of others. Social research has attached considerable significance to this process of shared understanding, and seeks to examine and understand how such 'meanings' are created.

Ultimately a great deal of social research attempts to understand the **world view** of respondents in research studies. The concept of one's world view is very broad, and embraces the entire range of ideas and understanding with which one looks at the world. It includes, for example, people's ideas about the origins of their culture and the way in which that culture is evolving. It embraces notions of norms and ethics, and the ideas people have about what is and what is not morally acceptable. Also included here are ideas about justice, about what should count as knowledge, and about how people should set about investigating the world. So wide is the concept of a world view that individuals may find it difficult to fully understand, or indeed explain, their world view to others. Nevertheless, it is a useful expression to use when writing about research, since it expresses in a straightforward manner the way in which an individual seeks to understand and attribute meaning to the world. Bulterman-Bos (2008) investigated the differing world views of teachers and researchers on the subject of education. She came to the conclusion that although such apparent differences were to some extent a result of the different roles of teachers and researchers, it was possible in principle to harmonize these differences.

Much research is also concerned with exploring the way in which human beings work together, and in effect, combine their world views into a cohesive whole. In the case of a school, for example, the teachers working there are all individuals with no doubt their own distinctive perspectives on the world, and yet they will largely manage to function together as a working unity. In other words, they will create a **social system**, which will be to a greater or lesser extent, successful in achieving its goals. It is perhaps not surprising that a great deal of research from a functionalist perspective is concerned with research into social systems, but other perspectives also address this issue. Various interpretive approaches seek to understand the mechanisms by which individuals work together within a system.

The concept of an **organization** is very closely related to that of a social system. They are both groups of people working together within a boundary, whether physical or representing a boundary of ideas, and also working towards the achievement of certain goals. As organizations are a feature of an industrial society, they have been the subject of much research. Their mode of operation is central to the effective functioning of, say, industrial production. Organizational psychology, for example, has been concerned with research into the way individuals interact within organizations, and in particular how they function together within hierarchical systems. The study of organizations is very relevant within our educational systems. The earliest form of education probably took the form of a one-to-one mentor arrangement, perhaps within the confines of the family. However, in a modern and postmodern society, the bureaucratization of education has led to the complex interplay of organizations and systems, each devoted to a separate aspect of the educational process, and often employing their own methodology.

The methodological framework

When expressing the aims and purposes of research it is usually necessary to articulate the broad methodology which will be employed. It will be important, for example, to distinguish between the aim of generating theory or of testing theory. The purpose of the research may be, on the one hand, to develop broad, general statements about the world, or to attempt to validate a previous assertion about the subject of the research.

Within an interpretive perspective the usual purpose of research is to create general statements about the world, or theories, which can normally be used to explain past observations and to predict future observations. A theory is developed from empirical data by means of the logical process of induction. The process whereby a theory is generated from observations is known as **theorizing**, and is an important element in interpretive research. Manning (2001) employed the dramatic elements in crime, to generate theory concerning the police in New York City, while Vaughan (2004) explored the theorizing process itself during an investigation of a disaster. Fook (2002) analysed the range of theorizing techniques in the context of social work research. As a final example, Lillis (2008) examined the nature of ethnographic theorizing in the exploration of academic writing.

A theory is generally assumed to have very broad applicability, extending perhaps even outside the confines of the earth. The atomic theory of matter is such a theory. It is assumed by scientists, that the atomic theory is applicable throughout the observable universe. It can be used to explain a wide variety of observations such as the freezing and boiling of liquids. However, it is conceivable that one day observations will be made which simply cannot be explained by the atomic theory, with the result that the theory will have been **falsified**, or shown not to apply in all situations. In such a case the theory will have to be modified. A theory is provisionally regarded as representing reality, until such a time as it might be falsified. An **hypothesis** does not have this degree of status. It is an estimate of the kind of observations the researcher thinks will be made in the future. If such observations are indeed found, then the hypothesis has been supported. If an hypothesis is supported on a number of different occasions then it may be gradually expanded into a theory. In the physical sciences, theories tend to be rather more certain than in the social sciences. In the former relatively few variables are involved, while in the social or human sciences the large number of variables makes it more likely that theories will require regular amendment. Tate (2008) studied the way in which two areas were trying to improve their economic infrastructure. In particular he researched the geographical factors which had an effect upon this process. He noted that some writers develop theories linking government intervention with success in achieving goals in local contexts.

In the social sciences we sometimes read the expression **grand theory**. This is a theory, but one which has a particularly broad range of applicability. A theory in the physical sciences, such as the theory of gravity for example, is assumed to operate throughout the universe. On the other hand theories in the social sciences are usually much more limited in terms of their sphere of influence. These may only be developed in relation to a restricted social group, and hence can only be expected to predict events within that context. However, there are theories within the social sciences which can be considered to operate on a much broader scale, comparable to the situation in the physical sciences. In economics, for example, the labour theory of value – which relates the value of a commodity to the value of the human effort expended in its production – can be considered as a grand theory, being in principle applicable in a wide range of situations.

The idea of **generalization** is very important in research. In virtually all research contexts, it is important to have an idea of the extent to which the conclusions may be considered applicable in other situations. This is important in survey research where a sample is drawn from a larger group of people or situations. In that case, the researcher usually wishes to estimate the extent to which conclusions drawn about the sample can be applied to the broader group of people. Even in the case of life history research where indepth data may be gather from just one respondent, the researcher will normally wish to form a view of the extent to which the conclusions might apply to other people with a similar background. Ultimately the purpose of all research is to estimate, as precisely as possible, the extent to which the findings can be applied or are relevant to other situations. Generalization may not be specifically included in the aims of a research project, but nevertheless it remains an implicit goal.

Other important aspects of the aims of research include **explanation** and **prediction**. The former is extremely difficult to achieve in social science research, simply because of the potentially large number of variables. It may possibly be easier to predict future events from research conclusions, particularly if a similar context is selected. However, this does not imply that the mechanism for one event following another is understood. Some research aims to collect data concerning an existing social theory, and in effect to test that theory. Such **validation** can be a legitimate aim in research. It is important, as noted above, that researchers do attempt to falsify theories. If the falsification process fails, and hence the theory is provisionally supported, we can speak of a provisional validation of the theory.

Finally, a term which is widely used in a variety of contexts in research is **argument**. This is used to refer to a logical series of premises in research, which in principle is subject to falsifiability. In general terms it might be used as an approximate synonym for 'proposition'. One would speak of 'testing' an argument or perhaps of 'validating' an argument or 'falsifying' an argument. As the word can be used in a variety of contexts, it can be useful to employ in research writing.

Points to consider

It is possible in research to use the word 'argument' in its more everyday sense as indicating a dispute or disagreement. One might say, 'there is an argument among academics concerning the relevance of that concept'. However, one might more usually write 'there is a lack of agreement' or 'there is a lack of consensus' rather than speaking of an argument.

Summary

This chapter has explored the use of a range of terms and concepts in discussing the formulation of research aims. The latter are an essential part of any research study since they will form the basis for the future research design. The precise wording of the aims determines the overall strategy for the research, including for example the type of data collection procedure. Finally, the aims are normally revisited in the conclusion of a study, to determine the extent to which they have been met.

 **Further reading**

Bailey, R. (ed.) (2009) *The Sage Handbook of Philosophy of Education*. London: SAGE.

Berry, R. (2004) *The Research Project: How to write it* (5th edn). Abingdon, Oxon: Routledge.

Provenzo Jr, E.F. (ed.) (2008) *Foundations of Educational Thought*. London: SAGE.

Torrance, H. (ed.) (2009) *Qualitative Research Methods in Education*. London: SAGE.

4

Analysing Previous Research

Chapter objectives

This chapter will help you to:

- Discuss academic literature which has a sociological perspective.
- Evaluate academic literature which employs psychological concepts.
- Analyse literature which contains a variety of theoretical perspectives.

Terms used

The following terms are used in this chapter: androcentricity; authority; collective consciousness; conscientization; critical theory; culture; deconstruction; dehumanizing; dominant culture; emancipation; empowerment; ethnicity; feminism; gender; humanistic psychology; ideology; individual consciousness; Marxism; masculinism; oppression; phenomena; power; praxis; race; reflective practice; self-actualization; social psychology; social reality; socio-economic status; sociology of knowledge; stereotype.

Discussing literature with a sociological perspective

Much research assumes that there exists in society phenomena which we can measure, investigate and explore, and which are as real as the ideas which we carry in our own minds. Thus if we consider the concept of social mobility, we will tend to have a shared understanding with others that there is a definite process whereby people can 'improve' themselves in society. For this concept to be meaningful, we need to hold a number of related ideas. There is first of all the concept of the existence of social strata. People 'belong' to certain social groups, with a certain status in society. This might be reflected in terms of their type of employment, and also in terms of their cultural activities. In addition there is the idea that these social strata differ in desirability and status, and that it is generally better to belong to a higher rather than a lower social stratum. It is generally assumed that people in a higher social stratum will have more desirable jobs, and will be paid more. They will therefore be able to purchase a better standard of living and quality of life to people in a lower social stratum. Finally in this complex interplay of ideas, we have the idea of social mobility, whereby we assume that it is possible in theory to move from a lower to a higher social stratum. This might be through the medium of education or through individual effort and initiative, by for example, entrepreneurial activity in developing a successful business. There is also the related aspiration, that having improved the social group or stratum to which we belong, our children will naturally belong to that new social stratum, and will not have to go through the same process of social advancement as we did. Now the interesting aspect of this is that we operate in our daily lives as if these ideas are 'real', or in other words, that they represent a **social reality**. We operate as if there really are these strata in society, and that they exist almost as if we could see them and touch them. They appear to have the status of empirical realities.

Such alleged social realities have important consequences for our lives. Some people will spend a great deal of time considering their status in society, and the ways in which it might be improved. They will act in every way as if social mobility is an absolute reality. It is perhaps interesting that in much research those conducting it do not pause to either consider or question the ontological status of the concepts which they are investigating. Perhaps it is better in some ways that they do not do so, since they might never progress to carrying out their research! However, it is still of interest that to all intents and purposes we will tend not to question the reality of the entities which we research. Instead we will take them for granted, and accept their existence.

The idea that all knowledge is developed within a social context is often known as the **sociology of knowledge** perspective, and was popularized, as noted earlier, by Berger and Luckmann (1967). It does however contain an inherent logical problem, which can be difficult to address. The central issue is that if we assume that all knowledge arises in a particular social context, and is dependent on that social situation for its origin, then the very notion of a sociology of knowledge must also arise within a particular social context. All our knowledge becomes dependent upon the prevalent state of society, and we are left with no absolutes to cling on to. All of knowledge is therefore relative, and entirely dependent upon the varying social circumstances of the period. For researchers, this viewpoint will not necessarily result in any problems, but it will engender a view of knowledge, that it is always developing and changing. When a researcher draws conclusions from an investigation then these must always be regarded as provisional, and subject to the possibility of change.

The notion of change is not quite so prominent with another sociological concept, that of **ideology**. This is a very interesting and important concept within sociological thought, and one which has a significant impact in a research concept. An ideology is a way of thinking about an aspect of the social world. It carries the implication, first of all, that it is fairly inclusive and relevant to a broad area of one's existence. Thus if we say that someone subscribes to a particular political ideology, then the assumption is that this influences a considerable part of their lives. Ideologies are also usually normative, in that they are associated with particular value systems. If we know the ideology to which a person subscribes, then we may feel reasonably confident that we can predict the way in which they will react to certain circumstances or events.

Depending to some extent upon the individual point of view, ideologies may be viewed in a slightly negative light. Indeed, to say that someone has a viewpoint which is ideological may be considered to be a slightly pejorative remark. The reason for this is that the concept tends to carry the implication of believing something unshakeably and to the exclusion of other viewpoints. Thus if we say that someone believes in a particular religious ideology, it rather carries the suggestion that they believe something so firmly that it excludes the possibility of thinking that someone else's views may be of interest or even, say, partially true. The concept of ideology carries this notion that there is only one true way of looking at something. Moreover, it is difficult in any absolute sense to verify, confirm or validate ideologies. Ultimately, as individual human beings we have a choice over which ideology to select, that is assuming that we wish to live by a specific framework of thought. In other words, it is very difficult to say that one ideology is superior to another, simply because they contain within them a subjective element about the nature of the world, and how best to address the subject of existence in that world.

The issue of an ideology can also affect the way in which research is conducted, since it is at least arguable that all research is to some extent ideological. When researchers plan a research design they will approach this task from the perspective of their accumulated learning up until that point. That accumulated learning may derive from their formal education, but also from informal learning experiences within their family and with friends. All of that learning can be regarded as constituting a form of ideology. Even an education in the liberal arts, designed partly to open the learner up to new ideas and approaches, can be regarded as a form of ideology, to the extent that it represents a particular *modus operandi* for examining the world. Many researchers will choose not to address this question of personal ideology when conducting research, and will assume it is self-evident that they are acting as objective researchers. Others, on the other hand, will try to subject their personal ideology to scrutiny and will even state this near the beginning of the study. For example, if research is conducted within a Marxist perspective, using as an analytic tool the differentials in society between those owning capital and those selling their labour, then it helps to state this near the beginning of the book or journal article. The reader can then interpret and understand the research within an ideology of that type. Much the same applies with feminist or masculinist research, where a gender-oriented ideology may be used to analyse data. In that case again, it is useful if the reader is aware of the ideological approach from the beginning.

Like many social science concepts, that of ideology is subject to a variety of slightly-different interpretations, depending upon one's particular viewpoint. Chiapello (2003) discusses two different approaches to understanding ideology, and looks at the use of the term within the perspective of Marx. She notes, for example, that Marxists will tend to view the theories of Marx as the only scientific explanation of the functioning of society. Dobles (1999) also discusses the concept of ideology within a Marxist perspective, asserting the importance of ensuring that the ideology of capitalism is not reproduced between generations, thus avoiding a consideration of the exploitative nature of the free market system.

> **?** **Questions to consider**
>
> When reading research reports or listening to a presentation it is always worth being 'critical' in terms of potentially ideological perspectives. Ask yourself:
>
> - Are any of the ideas in this research taken for granted, or assumed to be true?
> - Is the researcher approaching the research from a preconceived viewpoint?
> - Has the researcher been sufficiently challenging of him or herself in terms of the research design?

The study of ideology is sometimes related to the concepts of **power** and **authority** in society. Those who are in a position to define what will be perceived as the dominant ideology in a society are often in a position to exercise power. The dominant ideology specifies the ideas and concepts which are held to be important. If a person or organization is seen as the originator and interpreter of those ideas, then de facto, they possess a degree of power in that society. If there are disputes about the nature of those dominant, influential ideas, then they are the ones to whom people turn for advice or to re-define the nature of the ideology. This is the concept of knowledge being associated with power. However, if those same individuals are in a position to impose that ideology on others, and to establish that ideology as the most influential world view throughout society, then they are also in a position to exercise considerable power.

We will frequently see this type of process in operation when the head of an organization changes, and the new post holder changes the priorities of that organization. In effect, the new senior executive will re-define the dominant ideology of the organization. A new head teacher may decide to place a great deal of emphasis upon parental involvement in a school, or alternatively may make a special effort to encourage pupils to contribute to the local community. The authority vested in the role of the head teacher may be used to influence a change of direction in the philosophy of the school. Nevertheless, the school's staff are not without power themselves. The head teacher will require their support of the staff to put this change of ideology into place, and without that support the policy could never be totally successful. In some forms of organization, notably those where an autocracy prevails, the power to enforce an ideology may be very localized and vested in a single person, whereas in more democratic systems power is more distributed, and a greater degree of consensus may be required.

Concepts of power and ideology are of interest to researchers because they are central to an understanding of the way organizations function. They are relevant not only in schools, but also in hospitals, local authorities, and in private sector commercial organizations. Researchers are often interested in the way in which decisions are taken in organizations, and the mechanisms by which new policies are implemented. It is also interesting to investigate the way in which groups of individuals either come to accept a new ideology, or indeed work together to try to challenge a new world view. In both cases the process will often involve considerable inter-personal negotiation and discussion, and the nature of this is interesting to researchers.

The concept of power within organizations and hierarchies is interesting, and has important consequences for the behaviour of individuals within such organizations. Van Dijke and Poppe (2007) studied the preferences of respondents in terms of the power they would prefer to have within a hierarchy. Maner et al. (2007) examined the possible relationship between the power possessed by someone within a hierarchical structure, and the amount of risk associated with their decision making. The two variables appeared to be connected, along with a further variable of the extent to which the existing power distribution within the hierarchy was perceived as likely to alter in the near future.

The notion of power is also related to that of **empowerment**. Power is not evenly distributed in society. Some groups or individuals will accrue power by means of knowledge, wealth, or traditional authority, while others may have to develop power through cooperative social action. Many individuals or groups in society are however seen as lacking power, and a sense of decision making in relation to their own lives. In such cases, we will often speak of the process of empowerment, whereby they may be able to gradually gain a sense of control over their lives and to acquire the ability to influence the decision-making processes in society.

This process of empowerment may involve a number of different facets. In the initial stages it may include, at least partially, a change of psychology in terms of developing the self-belief that change in society is possible. This may also involve a process of self-education. As the process proceeds it may also involve a gradual appreciation of the way in which decisions are taken in society, and the mechanisms – for example through the mass media – by which the dominant ideology may be influenced by pressure groups. Researchers might wish to explore the various ways in which empowerment operates in society. The process may be multi-faceted, in that it is difficult for a community or social group to develop a sense of empowerment if they are living in unsatisfactory housing, with an inadequate diet and without access to good educational and health care systems. Perhaps above all, the educational system has a key role to play in the empowerment process, since without an understanding of society and how it can in principle be changed, it is difficult to challenge and improve the prevailing system.

Interestingly, McQuillan (2005) argues that the school system in the United States tends to socialize young people into being relatively passive, and hence does not equip them to be able to take a full part in the democratic processes of society. He suggests that such students do need to be empowered in order to be able to appreciate their future role in a democracy. Somech (2005) also noted the importance of the empowerment of work-based teams in educational contexts, and the positive effect that this could have on the empowerment of individual teachers.

The concept of **oppression** is often used to describe the process whereby a social group is excluded from the main ideological system of a society, and hence disenfranchised. There are unfortunately all too many cases where this happens around the world on a political level, but there are also other contexts in which the word may be used where the oppressive process may be far more subtle. For example, in some areas of the educational system it may be argued that the curriculum reflects middle-class values, and hence does insufficient work to demonstrate a sense of worth for working-class culture. It could also be argued that in such cases young people may become alienated from the educational system and demonstrate a systematic underachievement. Where this is alleged to have occurred we might speak of a form of cultural oppression, which should be rectified at least in part through a process of empowerment.

Shah and Nah (2004) examined the contexts in which certain events had been described by journalists as 'racial oppression'. In other words, when a particular news story is examined and researched by journalists, they do have a choice as to whether or not to describe it as featuring racial oppression. Evidently much of this would focus upon the concept of racial oppression which is held by the journalist. This is an important issue since the decisions which are taken may influence others and their perception of contemporary events. Schiele (2005) investigated the nature of cultural oppression in relation to African Americans, and concluded that such forms of oppression could have an adverse effect upon their social advancement.

Issues of oppression and empowerment have been discussed and researched widely in terms of **race** and **ethnicity**. Research has been conducted in the areas of discrimination and racism, and the ways in which these forms of oppression affect the life chances of individuals. Research on ethnic groups raises a number of interesting questions, not least of which is the issue of definition.

A number of different terms will be employed by researchers when referring to ethnic groups, including, for example, 'ethnic minority', 'black', terms such as 'Asian' which indicate a very broad geographical origin, and 'Afro-Caribbean' which imply both a geographical and cultural origin, in this case in Africa. There are also other terms which will indicate the religious backgrounds of a group, particularly where that is a significant component of the cultural heritage of a group of people. In other words, there is an extensive terminology which is employed by researchers when writing of ethnic groups, and this terminology is at times less than precise. While it is generally very important for researchers to be careful about the use and definition of concepts, this is even more important in this complex area.

The terms 'minority ethnic group' or 'ethnic minority' are frequently used by researchers, but as the migration to western countries has increased and 'minority' populations have become well-established, former minority communities have, in places, become 'majority' communities. To some extent then, the original term of choice has become imprecise and redundant. A new range of research issues has therefore become important, including for example, the changing nature of communities, as a new ethnic or religious group to some extent displaces the indigenous group in a particular locality. The term 'multi-cultural' has also been used in this kind of context, although it has been associated in the eyes of some with a consensus view of society, which tended to ignore the inequalities associated with race in society, and the racism within both society in general and some organizations in particular. The term 'multi-ethnic' has also faced some of the same criticisms, implying to some that there exists a degree of integration in society which is not felt to exist. The term 'multi-racial' faces the same criticism.

Indeed the concept of race itself has been challenged, on the grounds that some feel the category has no valid existence within human society, and that its alleged genetic basis is flawed. The current consensus appears to be that the notion of race is inappropriate, and indeed it has no biological basis. Originally, attempts were made to link the idea of human 'races' with physical appearance and skin colour, and to assume that there was a genetic basis to such differences of appearance. The accepted view now tends to be that there are more appropriate and accurate terms to describe categories of human beings, for the purposes of research. However, strangely perhaps, given the general discrediting of the term, it remains in such composite forms as 'racial discrimination' and UK legislation such as 'The Race Relations Act'.

As a means of differentiating human beings, the concept of 'ethnicity' seems to be generally preferred. An ethnic group is a group of people who share certain features, including perhaps a common language, a common cultural history, and may be also such features as religion, employment patterns, literature, music and art. These shared features will not be the same in different groups, but there will normally be some of these characteristics which can link people together. Ultimately however, researchers will usually be interested in dividing and distinguishing human beings, because they wish to investigate the possibility that membership of a particular group might be a significant variable. In other words, being a member of a particular group can result in changes in one or more other variables in the research study. When considering which categories of people to include in a research study, it is important that one thinks carefully about the purpose of the research. For example, if religious belief is an important variable, then it is important to take that into account into distinguishing people. All too often, research studies will select a nomenclature such as 'Asian' or 'migrants from the Indian sub-continent' without the researcher being very clear about the most precise type of category needed. For example, if religion is an important consideration, then clearly there are a number of different religions represented in the sub-continent of India. It might be more precise and appropriate to the research study to specify 'Indian Muslim' or 'Hindu' or 'Parsee'. Such descriptors would be much more precise than using terms such as 'Asian'.

Generally speaking in social research, the most important criterion for the choice of a category to describe respondents is that the category is related precisely to the aims of the study. Thus, if one were gathering data from a sample of Hindus, it may be important to recognize when designing the research that India is a very diverse country, and that there may be considerable cultural and linguistic variations between a Hindu from Calcutta and a Hindu living in Rajasthan. Similarly, although Muslims from Algeria, Syria and Malaysia will all share the key principles of Islam, nevertheless there will inevitably be some cultural variations between the three countries. Moreover, when researching race and ethnicity there is always the possibility that any factors which we think may be associated with membership of a particular ethnic group may in fact be more closely related to a factor such as social class. This discussion tends to suggest therefore, that we need to give considerable thought to the categories which we propose in research studies.

Much social research for example has been devoted to examining apparent differences between various ethnic groups in terms of educational performance. This is clearly an important issue in many countries which have diverse populations, and where there is a concern to ensure that all groups in society have access to the opportunities that allow for a progression in life. There is also the concern that forms of discrimination, however subtle and indirect, may militate against such progress. However, as with all forms of social research of this type, there may be factors such as language which are more important than the membership of an ethnic group. If, say, English is only the second language for a particular ethnic group, then this may have a considerable effect upon their educational attainment. Moreover, an issue such as **socio-economic status**, may in reality be more significant in terms of educational attainment than ethnicity. If a community is working hard to establish itself economically, it may not have the time, energy and resources to give as much advice and encouragement to children in school.

The concepts of race and ethnicity have been the subject of many research studies. Anagnostou (2009) considered the notion of 'symbolic ethnicity' which relates to the notion of individualism in American society, and the process whereby people from, say, diverse cultural and ethnic backgrounds may select the ethnicity with which they prefer to be associated. Smart et al. (2008) looked at the debate between a genetic definition of race and ethnicity and a social interpretation of the concepts. They noted the complexity of this debate, and that there is still evidence of the validity of a genetic understanding of race and ethnicity. Chandra and Wilkinson (2008) also noted the complexity of the term 'ethnicity', and the difficulties of employing it as a social science research variable. As part of the continuing debate about the concept of race, Sundstrom (2002) explored the ontology of the concept. Finally, in these examples of contemporary research on race and ethnicity, Mahtani (2002) examined the nature of the term 'mixed race' and the way in which it is conceptualized in society. Overall, these are concepts which continue to interest social scientists, and yet which, even from the point of view of having adequate definitions, are clearly problematic.

One of the commonest terms employed in social science research literature is that of **culture**. This term may be used in several different ways. The more general use is to refer to those broad aspects of art, philosophy, economics and social organization which can give a distinctive quality to a society. Thus we may speak of European culture or American culture. However, the concept can also be used in a narrower sense to refer to, for example, the culture of an organization such as a school. It is in this sense that it is often used extensively in research. In the case of a school we will tend to use the term to indicate the wide range of educational and organizational systems, of teacher attitudes and approaches, and of the management styles, which will collectively give the school a distinctive feature. The impact of such a culture on pupil attainment has also been of interest to educational researchers. In addition, however, there are a number of concepts used in research, which amplify and extend that of culture. In some societal contexts or in the case of organizations, we may speak of the **dominant culture**. Thus in an organization, we might speak of a person-centred management style as representing the dominant culture of the organization.

Culture, like ethnicity, has remained a central concept in social science research. Markowitz (2004) discussed the continuing importance of culture in the way in which people view themselves and make statements about how they conceive of themselves in contemporary society. At the same time it was argued that it may be necessary to amend somewhat the use of the concept to reflect the needs of current research. Garland (2006) noted the importance of culture in contemporary discussions about the nature of punishment, from both an individual and institutional perspective. Overall, such sociological concepts are central to research in social science, and hence are frequently found in the literature. When analysing previous research in any field in the social sciences, it will frequently be necessary to reflect on the relevance of at least some of these concepts. Nevertheless, other terms arising from a personal or more psychological perspective are also relevant when reviewing research literature.

Discussing literature with a psychological perspective

One of the main disciplines which links psychology and sociology is **social psychology**. As a discipline and area of research it tends to explore the relationships between individuals when they are working together or existing in groups. In any situation where colleagues work together in teams, the insights of social psychology will become significant. Equally in education, it has been an important discipline in terms of investigating the relationships between pupils in classrooms, and between teachers in staffrooms. In all social contexts there is a tension between the individual perception of the situation and the way in which the individual would wish to behave, and the pressures of the group which can tend to influence individual behaviour. Our working life will very often be a compromise between the priorities of the individual, and the demands of the social group. Social psychology has generated an enormous quantity of research during a relatively short time. Hill (2006), for example, discusses the way in which social psychology theory may be applied to some of the major contemporary social issues. Stam (2006), on the other hand, has examined the nature of the discipline of social psychology, and analysed some critiques of the field. Crandall and Schaller (2001) studied critiques of the nature of scientific enquiry in the field of social psychology, and tried to clarify the purpose and methodology of research within the field.

The way in which individual human beings perceive the world is often expressed using terms such as the **individual consciousness**. Most individuals however, while possessing a personal view of the world, will belong to a variety of social groups which will share certain values and norms. These social groups have therefore a form of **collective consciousness**. For example, individual teachers may have their own career aspirations, their own philosophy of education, and their own preferred teaching and learning techniques, but at the same time they will belong to a collective group of professionals with a number of shared concerns. Teachers in general at any particular time may be concerned about contractual issues, about national pay negotiations, about new government initiatives in education, and about trends in national exam results. These kind of concerns may help to shape the collective consciousness of the teaching profession.

The study of the individual and society has been the story of an extended debate about the importance of the individual on the one hand, and the way in which people shape their own lives, and on the other hand, the significance of the collective, and the way in which groups and society can affect the individual. The French sociologist Emile Durkheim attached great significance to the role of the collective, as have those sociologists who have broadly adopted a structuralist view of society. Ultimately there is no way of resolving this debate, since both the individual and the collective are important in shaping society. Research studies will often have to focus on one or the other approach, since to address all possible influences in one study might be too complex.

A discipline which has focused upon the individual consciousness is that of **humanistic psychology**. Evolving in the 1950s, it owed much of its early development to the psychologists Abraham Maslow and Carl Rogers. The discipline concentrated its attentions upon the needs and development of the individual human being. Central among its ideas was that of the way in which individuals strive to achieve both a sense of personal fulfilment and their full potential. Such **self-actualization** became a key concept of the discipline. In reality, the needs and pressures of the group may militate to some degree against the individual being able to fully self-actualize. For example, an individual employee may wish to undergo additional professional training in an area which interests them, but their employer may not be able or willing to finance such professional development. In many situations, the social groups to which we belong may both assist and hinder our capacity to fulfil ourselves and to self-actualize. Diaz-Laplante (2007) discusses the extent to which humanistic psychology can be applied to contexts other than that of helping the individual, particularly in an economically-developed western situation. In particular she is interested in the application of the principles of the discipline to the context of extremely under-developed countries, in order to help the rural poor. Cain (2003) examined the current state of humanistic psychology as a discipline and the extent to which it is expanding in influence. Joy (2005) explored the way in which the insights and ethics of humanistic psychology may be employed to encourage a more ethical treatment of animals. Finally Giorgi (2005) reminded us of the original context in which humanistic psychology provided us with a different model for psychological research than the prevalent positivistic one of the period.

The idea of self-development has become increasingly enshrined in professional practice within a number of different occupations, notably within the professions of health and education. In particular the philosophy of **reflective practice** has been extensively advocated, and has become an intrinsic part of many programmes of professional development. In education, for example, teachers are encouraged to reflect upon their practice in the classroom, and to consider ways in which it could be improved and developed. Such reflection is envisaged as taking place not only during a period of teaching or professional activity, but also when it has been completed. The idea of such reflection is that it provides ideas for the improvement of professional practice, which can then inform and help the next teaching session. There then exists a continuous feedback loop, which can improve practice. It is also necessary sometimes to include a professional friend who can engage in dialogue with the person undertaking the reflection, and assist them in addressing appropriate questions about the practice. This type of activity has been the subject of considerable research.

However, in the process of reflection, we cannot be sure that each individual professional is perceiving the same entity as someone else. Two teachers in the same classroom may 'see' aspects of pupil behaviour in very different ways. One may see a pupil as disruptive and aggressive, while the other teacher may see that pupil as simply boisterous. In a hospital, one doctor may explain symptoms in one way, and a different doctor may interpret things in a different way. In other words, **phenomena**, or observable events, may be interpreted in very different ways. Within psychology, phenomenology is thus often concerned with understanding the nature of individual meaning, and the way in which meanings are attributed to events.

The interpretation of the psychological and other characteristics of social groups may lead to the development of **stereotypes**. These are generalizations which are assumed to apply to all members of a social or, for example, ethnic group. Every member of the group is assumed to possess those general qualities. Stereotypes are typically negative, although sometimes may represent positive characteristics. There is usually no valid evidence to assume that alleged characteristics actually do apply to all members of the social group, or that alleged characteristics do not also apply to other groups. Stereotypes thus represent a logical fallacy of unwarranted generalization, and in the case of negative stereotypes, malign individuals through assuming that they possess negative characteristics simply by virtue of belonging to a particular social group.

Questions to consider

Stereotypes are fundamentally irrational, because they are not based upon complete evidence. They may be partially true of some members of a social group, but that is insufficient to warrant a generalization. When reading research reports ask yourself:

- Is the researcher making any assumptions here which are not justified by the evidence?
- Are there any generalizations about a social group, based on only limited evidence?

Discussing literature with a theoretical perspective

The idea of human beings trying to self-actualize is also present in a number of other concepts. A particularly well-known example is the term **conscientization** which was first used by the Brazilian educator and social reformer, Paulo Freire. Much of his philosophy of education which he described in his book *Pedagogy of the Oppressed*, was concerned with his attempts to increase literacy levels among the rural poor in Brazil. In so doing however, he was not concerned exclusively with literacy levels per se, but with the improved levels of self-determination which he hoped would accompany the ability to read and write. He wanted the Brazilian peasants with whom he worked to be able to use their new-found literacy to understand more of the political and economic system within which they lived, and hence to be able to argue for reforms in society to improve their lives. The term 'conscientization' implied a deeper understanding of the way in which society functioned and of their place within it. Moreover, it implied an increasing ability to transform their own lives and the place of their communities within society.

Although derived from a Portuguese word, and used originally in a South American context, the basic concept of conscientization can also be applied more generally to other parts of the world where the poor have apparently little capacity to control and improve their own lives.

It is an idea which is related to the previously-mentioned concept of empowerment, but also to the idea of **emancipation**. The latter is the concept of giving or gaining freedom for those who for some reason do not possess autonomy. It may apply to individuals, sub-groups or even to an entire community or society. Emancipation may also refer to a situation where people do not have the right to vote in democratic elections, and have little control over their economic and political destinies. They may have inadequate health care, and lack access to an adequate educational system. Just as conscientization is linked to the idea of fulfilling one's potential through education, so emancipation is a concept which may be used in educational research contexts to suggest the use of education for social reform and the generation of freedom of action for individuals. It has a particular connection to the ideas of female emancipation and **feminism**.

Feminist theory and feminist perspectives have inspired a wide range of social research. Feminist researchers have argued that much of social research is male dominated, both in terms of the subjects which have been selected for investigation, the perspectives with which they have been viewed, and also in terms of the methodologies which have typically been used as means of investigation. They have also argued that there has been insufficient attention given to the issues which affect women, such as a lack of equality in the workplace, a lack of recognition for the work which women perform in raising children and looking after the family, and a lack of acknowledgement of the ways in which women are disempowered in society. It has also been argued that in some ways it is difficult for men to research such issues adequately, since their role as men in society hampers their capacity to view such **gender-related** issues objectively. It is further argued by many feminist researchers that research in general is affected by gender, in terms of the types of methodology which are selected in order to investigate issues. It is suggested that male researchers, by virtue of a male-oriented view of the world, will typically select quantitative approaches which will attempt to express society in a manner that is typical of the physical sciences. Feminist researchers would argue that more qualitative methods are needed to give full expression to the feelings and world views of women. A view of the world which is distinctively male-oriented is often described as an **androcentric** view, or as reflecting a philosophy of **androcentricity**.

A good deal of gender-oriented research has focused upon the ways in which the education system is argued to have replicated gender differentiation in society, and in particular has disenfranchised girls through the types of curricular choices available to them. It has also examined the ways in which a lack of female role models among teachers in some subjects may have an adverse effect upon the career choices made by girls. Increasingly however, research has needed to address such issues as the under-performance of boys in some subjects, and this has initiated a range of **masculinist** research, motivated by the need to examine the issues in contemporary society which may differentially affect the education of boys.

There is an extensive range of social science research written either on feminism, or from a feminist perspective. Enslin (2003) has discussed the sometimes complex interaction between a liberal, feminist education and the perspective of multiculturalism, while Hayes et al. (2000) has examined the interface between the rise of post-war feminism and the move towards a postmaterialist value system. Sa'ar (2005) looked at the strategies employed by disadvantaged groups, including women, in relating to the liberal ideology of some dominant groups. Calloni (2003) on the other hand, examined the evolving role of feminist thought, particularly within a globalized society. Gambaudo (2007) interrogated the two categories of French feminist thought and Anglo-American feminist thought, while Harnois (2005) analysed the interface between race and gender on feminist roles.

Inequalities in our educational system have been researched from a variety of other perspectives besides that of gender. **Marxism**, as a political and economic philosophy, has motivated much research in terms of the functioning of the educational system. Marxist analysts have often viewed western educational systems as reflecting and reproducing the traditional class divisions of society. Through for example the nature of the curriculum, working-class children are perceived as exploited by the system, with little chance of demonstrating their intrinsic abilities, and being destined for the type of employment which casts them in the role of supporting the capitalist system. Working-class children are thus alienated from their true potential. Marxism as a world view emphasizes that it is important not only to analyse the true nature of the economic relationships in society, but also to actually change the capitalist system through **praxis**. In other words, it is important to transform society and within it the educational system by using the theoretical ideas within Marxism. Educational research inspired by Marxist perspectives has motivated educationalists to reconsider such issues as the types of curriculum offered in schools, the approaches to teaching, and the forms of assessment used, in order to encourage a greater element of equality.

Without such attempts to introduce more equality into the educational system, Marxists would view the alienation which it produces as being in effect **dehumanizing**, since it is argued that the a major section of society, notably the working classes, will be consigned to inferior and demeaning jobs. A social philosophy known as **critical theory**, associated with the so-called Frankfurt School of social theory, has sought to emphasize such a radical critique of society. Often inspired by a Marxist analysis, but also by other radical approaches, critical theory has stressed the need to change society in order to establish a fairer system and one which is more rooted in essentially human values. It is a wide-ranging and eclectic approach, which in some ways has provided a unifying theme for a number of different thinkers.

Finally, it is perhaps worth noting that many of the concepts mentioned so far in this book have related to the theme of social science research, that there are often many different ways of perceiving the same phenomenon. The argument that multiple perspectives exist in the world is a major theme of contemporary social science. When we are investigating an issue, we will often articulate the particular perspective we are using because implicit in the research process is the notion that there are other competing perspectives and world views. This idea is a central element in a much used contemporary term, that of **deconstruction**. Originally coming from the French philosopher Jacques Derrida, although rooted in earlier phenomenological theory, the term stresses the limitations of what is written about a subject. When we discuss or analyse something, the existence of an almost infinite range of possible perspectives means that there will almost inevitably be omissions in what we write. The purpose of deconstruction is that when we do read something, we should attempt to identify what is missing from the text. By deconstructing the text in this way, we are then actually able to learn more about the subject. In effect, we develop a more sensitized awareness of the subtleties and possible ways of thinking about a particular topic or idea.

▭ Summary

When reviewing published social science research, one can draw upon the full range of terms and ideas employed in the field. Nevertheless, this chapter has reviewed some of the concepts which may be particularly useful in this process. We may be interested, for example, in the way knowledge appears to be created within a particular area, and will thus employ a sociology of knowledge or social construction perspective. Certainly, we might also be interested in what a piece of research says about some of the key themes of social research such as inequality, class, race and gender, and also the nature of human beings. Finally, in reviewing research, we may wish to consider the extent to which research improves the world, or affects the lives of people, and here such concepts as empowerment, emancipation and reflective practice may be particularly significant. This chapter has tried to elucidate such terms and explain their potential use.

 **Further reading**

Breakwell, G.M. et al. (eds) (2006) *Research Methods in Psychology* (3rd edn). London: SAGE.

Fennell, S. and Arnot, M. (2007) *Gender, Education and Equality in a Global Context*. Abingdon, Oxon: Routledge.

Fink, A. (2008) *Practicing Research*. London: SAGE.

Green, J. and Thorogood, N. (eds) (2009) *Qualitative Methods for Health Research* (2nd edn). London: SAGE.

Tomlinson, S. (2008) *Race and Education: Policy and Politics in Britain*. Maidenhead: Open University Press.

5

The Scientific Method

Chapter objectives

This chapter will help you to:

- Understand the nature of the scientific method.
- Analyse the concept of social science.
- Appreciate some of the principal themes and ideas of social science.

→ Terms used

The following terms are discussed in this chapter: antipositivism; causal variable; dependent variable; descriptive statistics; emic; etic; experimental method; falsification; hypothesis; idiographic; independent variable; inferential statistics; interpretivism; key informant; law; methodological triangulation; natural science; nomothetic; non-probability sample; physical science; positivism; probability sample; purposive sample; sample; random sample; research population; science; scientific method; snowball sample; social science; staged sampling; statistical significance; stratified sample; survey research; theory; validity.

The method of science

The term **science** is very widely-used in both popular and academic contexts, and is frequently associated with the idea of research. The use of the term has, however, broadened considerably since it was first employed. In its most general sense, the concept of science involves a systematic and logical enquiry into something. For an enquiry to be considered scientific, there must be the assumption that it has been conducted in a thoughtful and planned way. A further aspect of science is that it is usually associated with those areas of human enquiry which are susceptible to the gathering and analysis of evidence. Some may argue, for example, that science is not appropriate for the resolution of questions concerning ethics. If someone were to propose that violence is wrong, then we might collect a great deal of evidence about violent incidents, but it may not be possible to decide finally on the question simply on the basis of this evidence. This is because ultimately the decision as to whether or not violence is wrong is a question of value and not of fact. The result is that science as a general discipline is usually not associated with such areas as religion and morality, where questions of value remain pre-eminent.

It is interesting, however, that the term 'science' has been applied in recent years to some areas such as the study of politics, where many questions are arguably questions of value. Thus we do hear the expression 'political science' used to describe the study of politics. Certainly one can gather a great deal of evidence in the realm of politics, such as economic data, demographic data, and evidence of the voting patterns of the electorate. Equally, that evidence can be used to support political decision making. However, ultimately, the evidence which is collected within the realm of politics may lead different individuals to arrive at very different conclusions, often based upon their personal political ideology. In other words, the political value system of an individual has a major effect upon conclusions drawn from the evidence. This perhaps calls into question the appropriateness of the term 'science' being applied to politics.

Points to consider

In research dissertations students will sometimes speak of their research being 'scientific', or that the data collection process was 'scientific'. However, as 'science' is a rather general term, such usage is fairly imprecise and perhaps better avoided. It merely begs a range of further questions such as 'What do you mean by "science" and "scientific"?'

The concept of science, is also found in the term **natural science**, **physical science**, and **social science**. The term 'natural science' is perhaps less used in contemporary contexts, but as its name suggests it refers broadly to the scientific investigation of the natural world, taken to include both the material aspects of the universe and also the living world. Hence it is also taken to include broadly such sciences as astronomy, geology, physics, chemistry, biochemistry, and the biological sciences. However, the term 'natural science' does have a slightly flexible useage, and may sometimes be applied simply to the natural world, suggesting the study of botany, animal behaviour, ecology, environmental studies, and zoology. In this more specific sense, natural science may be loosely equated with biological sciences.

The term 'physical science' is typically used to distinguish such disciplines as physics, chemistry, engineering, and the more specific subject areas associated with them, from the study of human beings and society known usually as the social sciences. The latter is normally taken to include the disciplines of sociology, psychology, and associated more specialist areas. The question arises, however, as to whether the physical sciences and the social sciences are both 'scientific' in the same sense. This is an interesting and complex issue, and probably not capable of being resolved entirely. In the looser, more general sense of 'scientific' they are certainly comparable in that they are equally committed to the logical, rational and systematic investigation of issues and problems. However, there are differences between the two disciplines in terms of the types of constraints which will operate when research is being conducted. In a physical sciences laboratory it is possible to control many of the potential variables within an investigation, whereas this is extremely difficult in investigations which encompass human beings and human communities. The result is that one can attempt the more precise, and usually quantitative, measurement of variables within physical science research, whereas in social science research the researcher will often have to collect data which, while more detailed, may be qualitative and, in a sense, less precise. However, in comparing the relative research approaches in the physical and social sciences, much will depend upon our definition of what constitutes the **scientific method**.

This approach to generating new knowledge about the world has evolved gradually, but also culminated in a logical approach to collecting and analysing data. In trying to resolve an issue or problem, the first stage is normally considered to be the generation of a **hypothesis**. This is a concise statement or proposition about the particular problem, which purports to explain that problem. In order to establish the validity or otherwise of this hypothesis, a researcher will then collect some data either through a laboratory experiment, field observation, or some other method. After analysis, a judgement will be made as to whether the data tend to support or negate the hypothesis. If the analysis negates the hypothesis, then the latter is amended and refined, and the process repeated until it appears that the hypothesis is indeed supported. In the latter case, a number of different hypotheses may be combined into a general statement about the world, or **theory**. Such an explanatory statement will normally have a wider applicability than a hypothesis.

However, this generation of a theory which appears to support the available data is not the final stage of scientific enquiry. There is the assumption within the scientific approach that all theories must remain essentially provisional. There always remains the possibility that new data will be obtained which will negate the theory. In addition, as a scientific theory is placed in the public domain, other researchers may use it to generate new hypotheses which will then be tested. Even more so, researchers will attempt to **falsify** the hypothesis, and hence the theory from which it derived. The use of this term 'falsification', rather than affirmation, emphasizes the sceptical nature of scientific enquiry. In other words, a researcher does not set out to prove something is true, but rather seeks evidence which will negate a proposition about the world. If such evidence is not available at that time, then at least the scientist can feel that everything possible has been done in terms of the rigour of the research.

In comparing research in the physical sciences with that in the social sciences, this general method tends to be employed in each. To that extent they are both scientific in their general approach and philosophy. However, there are matters of emphasis which do distinguish the two broad disciplines. In the social sciences, there tends perhaps to be rather less emphasis upon the generation and testing of hypotheses. A greater tendency to collect qualitative data will often result in researchers trying to generate a broad theory from such data, which might be used in the future to produce hypotheses. In the physical sciences, the greater degree of quantitative measurement which is available will tends to encourage the creation and testing of hypotheses, and this is often done through use of the **experimental method**.

The experimental approach probably reflects the nature of science more accurately than any other attempt to generate new knowledge about the world. It is essentially concerned with trying to determine the reasons for events taking place. In other words, it attempts to establish causal relationships or to determine what causes a particular event. The classic example of this approach is found in the physics or chemistry laboratory. We may be interested in exploring which factors affect the speed of a chemical reaction. Therefore we might change the acidity of the environment for that reaction, and see whether there is a change in that speed. In this example, the change in acidity is known as the **independent variable** (or sometimes the **causal variable**), and the speed of the chemical reaction is termed the **dependent variable**. The hypothesis here is that the dependent variable may change as the independent variable changes. However, in order to establish this with any degree of certainty it would be necessary to ensure that no other variables had changed during the experiment. It would thus be necessary, for example, to maintain a constant temperature throughout the experiment because this might be a significant causal variable itself.

This is the essence of the experimental method. However, it cannot yield results of absolute certainty. Despite all the best efforts of the experimenter, there may be variables which have not been totally controlled, or indeed variables of which the experimenter was unaware. Therefore it is always generally a good idea to try to repeat experiments as often as possible. The more an experiment is repeated by different experimenters, and the same or similar results obtained, then the more certain we can be that the original results were valid.

Social scientists have attempted to use this experimental approach in some areas, in order to recreate the apparent level of precision gained by physical scientists. Versions of the experimental method have been used in psychology, social psychology, and in education. While the method does lend itself to situations involving human beings, the added complexity of the situation often makes the results less certain. For example, we might consider a situation where we are trying to develop new methods of teaching foreign languages. Perhaps it is considered that the traditional method of teaching systematically the grammatical structures of the language is too slow and too uninteresting for many students. A new method may then be tried of simply exposing students to long periods of conversation in the same language, without any attempt to teach them the intricacies of its grammar. This new method would be the independent variable, while the level of competence achieved in the language would be the dependent variable. However, we could not be certain that any improvement in performance was due exclusively to the new method. Some students may be doing private study, of various kinds, which would affect their performance. The complexities of any context involving human beings make the experimental method difficult to apply with certainty. Nevertheless, given such caveats, it still remains a valuable technique for research.

A number of writers have commented specifically on the apparent reluctance of educationalists and educational researchers to employ experiments in education-based research. Cook (2002, 2003) has particularly discussed this issue, while Farrington (2003) has written on the general lack of use of the experimental method in criminology and Green and Gerber (2003) have noted the relatively infrequent use of field experiments in political science. However, some authors (see Gerber, 2004; Pager, 2007) have reported specifically on the use of field experiments. Finally, Nickerson (2006) used an experimental method to study the impact of phone calls on the participation of voters.

The concept of social science

One of the central methodological debates in the social sciences has been that between what is termed **positivism**, and its antithesis, **antipositivism**. In the mid-nineteenth century, the great rapidity of scientific and technological advance gave people enormous confidence in the methods of science. In France, the sociologist Auguste Comte was particularly well-known for advocating positivism – the view that empiricism and science were the way in which we could acquire knowledge about the world. He felt also that this was true not only of enquiry in the natural, physical world but also of enquiry in the social world. In other words, the methods of science could just as well apply in the laboratory as in the investigation of society. This approach held sway in the social sciences for a considerable time, and various attempts were made to quantify many aspects of society. Indeed we still see examples of this approach today, for example in education and the social sciences, where attempts are made, say, to compare quantitatively, schools or local authorities in terms of performance.

> **?** — **Questions to consider**
>
> Sometimes researchers will take rather fixed positions about the virtues of positivism on the one hand, and anti-positivism on the other. Rather than favouring one or the other, it is probably better to ask the following types of question:
>
> - Which approach is most suited to the aims of my research?
> - Which method can shed most light on the particular issue I am investigating?

Nevertheless, from the mid-twentieth century onwards, there was a tendency to point out some of the limitations of the positivist philosophy, and this became known as antipositivism. Positivists have generally felt that the scientific approach was the most appropriate method of enquiry, irrespective almost of the situation or context. On the other hand, antipositivists have also pointed out that there are distinctive features of human society which will result in the positivist approach not always being suitable. They would argue, for example, that when a researcher collects data from another human being that a certain amount of interpretation has to take place. They suggest that the data will not necessarily be available in a straightforward and precise form, and the researcher will have to make sense of the data before these can be used. This need to understand and make sense of data led to the development of the major perspective in sociology and social science research known as **interpretivism**.

In general, positivists tend to believe that there is a fundamental separation between the researcher and the object or phenomenon which is being investigated. In other words, a researcher can stand separately from the research context and observe it dispassionately and objectively. Thus the researcher is not really involved in the research context. Interpretivists, on the other hand, would take a rather different view. They conceive of the researcher and the object of research as being inextricably linked. In practice, this means that the object of research is perceived as being influenced by the researcher, and the latter in turn is affected by the research context. The social world is seen as embracing both the researcher and the object of the research. Within the interpretive understanding, the object of the research is thus understood through the consciousness of the researcher. The researcher has to understand and make sense of that which is being investigated.

Interpretivists are also rather sceptical of the quantitative approaches used by positivists. They feel that the process of quantification inevitably over-simplifies reality, and reduces the opportunities for research respondents to express the complexity of their feelings about the world. As a research method the social survey is, according to interpretivists, rather constraining. Respondents are given limited choices in terms of providing data, and have to find a way of responding to issues within the limitations of the questions. On the other hand, interpretivists feel that the methods typically used within the qualitative traditions of research, notably the interview, focus group or observational techniques, provide the respondent with much more opportunity to reflect their true feelings and opinions. The argument of interpretivists is that this increases the **validity** of the data.

The validity of research or data is the extent to which those data actually measure what they purport to measure. Alternatively, one could say that it is a measure of the extent to which the data represent the true feelings of the respondent. There are many factors in research which may limit the validity of data. It can be argued, for example, that all respondents whether operating within a qualitative or quantitative tradition, will try to present themselves in a certain way, which may not strictly-speaking represent the totality of their true views. Respondents may wish to represent simply one aspect of their views, or they might feel that the particular research context demands that they emphasize only one dimension of their thoughts. This might be particularly true, for example, when people are interviewed in a work context. Respondents may feel that they have obligations to their employer, and this may affect the way they present their responses. Another factor which can affect validity is our capacity to remember events. If we are asked, for example, to recall a specific event in the past, or perhaps to remember how frequently we have undertaken a specific action, the vagaries of our memory may affect the validity of the data we provide. Validity, then, is a concern for all researchers as they strive for as accurate a representation as possible between data and the reality which those data represent, and one of the most important factors in that representation is the manner in which data are collected.

Generally-speaking qualitative methods are associated with an interpretive perspective, since the latter relies on a level of detail, complexity, and sophistication in the data, in order to perform the interpretive process. On the other hand, positivism is associated with quantitative data since this perspective assumes a precision in terms of measuring social phenomena. There are other terms, however, which will be employed in discussing data and data collection. **Nomothetic** methods are those methods in research which attempt to represent the world in terms of scientific generalizations. They would normally employ quantitative measures, and seek to establish statistical probabilities. **Idiographic** methods, on the other hand, would typically employ approaches involving the collection of in-depth, qualitative data. Other related terms include **emic** and **etic**. A research account which is described as emic, generally derives from data obtained from within a social context. Such data are thus typically rather more subjective in character, and may reflect more personalized views and perspectives on issues. These are also more likely to be qualitative in nature, and to address issues which are more specific to that particular social context. On the other hand, etic accounts are generally produced by people who are external to the social situation. In that sense they are more likely to aspire to objectivity, and to attempt to draw comparisons with other social situations. The data of etic accounts may be quantitative or qualitative, but the tendency to draw comparisons and make generalizations tends to encourage the use of quantitative data.

Social science, just like the physical sciences, attempts to understand and describe the world. Although its subject matter is the complexity of human beings and human interaction, social science still attempts to generalize about the world, and to apply findings from one context in another situation. In other words, it seeks to make general statements about the world. The most straightforward scientific generalization about the world is probably the kind of statement known as a **law**. This is a succinct summary of the way in which events appear to take place in the world. By producing such a summary, a law also implicitly predicts the way in which events will occur in the future. As laws are such precise and relatively brief summaries, they are more typical of the physical sciences than the social sciences. They lend themselves to summary statements of the way in which scientific variables appear to interact. As social situations will often involve a greater range of variables a more complex generalization will often be needed, employing some form of explanation rather than a straightforward summary of the manner in which phenomena appear to interact. Such a more complex generalization is often known as a **theory**. The assumption behind a theory is that it is a well-established statement about the world, which has the support of a significant number of researchers. In this sense a theory differs somewhat from an hypothesis, which is only an assumption about the world. For an explanation to be termed a theory, there has to be an assumption that it is commonly regarded as at least provisionally true. The word 'provisionally' is used here because of the sense that a theory can always be revised and amended. The possibility will remain that someone will collect some data which will not fit with the theory, and in that case the only solution is to modify that same theory. Nevertheless, a theory remains probably the most sophisticated outcome of the scientific method, in that it represents the best way in which researchers can summarize the particular issue which they are investigating.

Themes of social science

The scientific method rests very much upon the process of careful research design. When one researcher is examining the results of another researcher, one of the first things they will be interested in is the way in which the research was planned. Central to this process in social science is the question of which people were chosen to provide data, and the important issue of the way in which they were chosen.

All research projects need to be sufficiently focused in order that they clarify to whom the research applies. If someone decides to conduct some research on high school teachers, they will need to be clear about whether they are interested in all high school teachers in a particular country or, say, high school teachers of a specific subject. They may in fact not be interested in all high school teachers in a country, but in teachers in a restricted range of schools. A research study of nurses may be specifically concerned with psychiatric nurses for example, or perhaps newly-qualified nurses. The group of people who are the focus of a research project are known as the **research population**. When the project is completed, and the results have been determined, the researcher will need to specify to whom the results are applicable. To put this another way, the researcher will be interested in the generalizability of the results. Normally, research results will be generalizable to the specified research population. This is not to say that the results cannot be generalized to anyone else, but simply that they may not be quite as applicable or relevant.

When a research project is being designed, however, a researcher may realize that it is not possible to collect data from the whole of the research population. The population may simply be too big, and it may not be practical to contact them all. It might be theoretically possible to send them all a questionnaire, but in practice this may be too expensive or involve too much administration. In other cases, the data collection method itself may make it impractical to contact all members of the research population.

Interview research, for example, is very time-consuming, and it would be impractical to contact each member of a large population. Sometimes also, the individual members of a research population may be difficult to identify with certainty. For example, if you wanted to identify high school teachers who were enrolled for a higher degree by part-time study, this might be slightly more difficult that it might seem at first sight. First of all, if the teachers are paying for the course themselves they may not have informed their employers. Equally, the university may not be permitted to disclose any information about individual students. The researcher may therefore only be able to identify a small number of members of the total potential research population. In all of these cases, the researcher would have to be satisfied with collecting data from a limited number of people. These would constitute the **research sample**.

The importance of a sample can often be seen most clearly in **survey research**. A survey is a research design which aims to collect data from a relatively large population, but where it is difficult in practice to contact all the population members. Therefore it is necessary to select a sample. A survey usually aims to collect a relatively small amount of data from each individual, but tries to collect those data from a large number of people. It is thus a research design which lends itself to monitoring or exploring large-scale trends. If the results from the sample are going to be generalizable to the whole survey population, then it is important that the sample is typical or representative of the population in terms of the latter's general characteristics. It is very difficult, if not impossible, to achieve this in practice, but the most effective approach is to employ a **probability sample**. This is a sample in which each member of the population has a known probability of being selected. It is often known as a **random sample**, and is usually selected by using lists of random numbers. As most surveys will adhere to a scientific or positivistic model of research, their ultimate purpose usually is to draw statistical inferences from the results. A probability sample is normally necessary for this to be accomplished with any validity. However, there are some potential difficulties with probability samples.

Sometimes a researcher might be interested in a particular category of individual in the population, because they reflect the variable which is a focus of the research. In a research study of nurses, it might be that the researcher is interested in any differences in approach or attitude between male and female nurses. If a simple random sample were drawn, there could – simply by an accident of sampling – be proportionately greater numbers of one gender than another in the sample. This need not necessarily be a drawback for the research, as it could be amended by using a **stratified sample**. In this case, suppose that a 10 per cent random sample was required. The population of nurses would be divided into two separate populations of male nurses and female nurses. Ten per cent of each group would then be selected randomly. By putting these two samples together, we would have an overall sample which reflected the proportion of males and females in the original population.

In another variant of probability sampling, we may need to collect data from the employees of a large organization, perhaps an international organization. In this case it may be impractical to access data from the entire research population. One might, for example, divide the organization into departments or functional units, and to begin with take a random sample of those. Then, in the next stage, one could take a random sample from those departments. This is sometimes known as **staged sampling**.

In a great deal of qualitative research, where there is a need to collect detailed data from respondents, it is often important to select a small sample of individuals who are both able and willing to provide these type of data. They need to have the kind of detailed knowledge of the research issue which enables them to provide in-depth data. In addition, as the data collection procedure can often be time-consuming they must be prepared to devote such time to the research. These requirements mean that a simple random sample may not be the most appropriate method, as it might not identify such people. Other forms of selection, often known as **non-probability sampling** or **purposive sampling**, must be used here. The necessity is often to identify people termed **key informants**, who have specialized knowledge or experience of a question. On occasion, it may not be possible to identify individuals who are members of a particular research population. For example, in a qualitative study of teachers who are unhappy with their job, and would like to change profession, it may be difficult to identify respondents because they prefer to present themselves at work as committed and dedicated professionals. They may only tend to discuss such reservations in private, among other people who they suspect of having similar feelings. In such a case, having identified perhaps one such respondent that person may be able to suggest another who could be contacted by the researcher. From then on, respondents may be identified by personal recommendation. This is often known as **snowball sampling**.

\|
o   **Points to consider**

Just as a rolled snowball accumulates more snow, the idea of snowball sampling is that respondents are gradually accumulated by personal reference. However, there are clear limitations here. A researcher will clearly be dependent upon the chain of relationships established by those who know each other. Such respondents are clearly self-selecting, and may not be representative.

Social science research is often portrayed as being a rigid division between qualitative methods or quantitative methods. This then appears as being an almost ideological divide between researchers. However, it is perhaps more appropriate to think of the specific requirements of a research question. In other words, when we establish the aims of a research project, the principal issue is the research strategy which can best be used to fulfil those aims. Indeed there may be occasions when a combination of qualitative and quantitative methods may be the most appropriate. Such multi-method approaches may provide a form of **methodological triangulation** which is not only more relevant to the needs of the particular research issue, but also helps to ensure greater validity of the data and findings.

Qualitative research methods, as a generality, tend to be more concerned with theory generation using, for example, grounded theory approaches, while quantitative research methods are more concerned with theory testing using statistical approaches. It is important when discussing the use of statistics not to employ language which implies a greater level of certainty about the conclusions drawn than is justified. In everyday and popular language there is often a greater degree of reliance placed upon findings involving numerical data than should be warranted. Statistics are often used for two distinct purposes. They can be used first of all for summarizing social science data. Thus, we might use statistics to summarize demographic data about population trends and present this in, for example, tabular form. Such numerical data simply attempt to present information in a logical form which can be readily understood, and is often known as **descriptive statistics**. It does not attempt to suggest anything about the relationships between the different categories of data, but simply to be concerned with the presentation of the data. However, statistics are also used to try to establish relationships or connections between variables. They are used to estimate, for example, whether a change in one variable may be caused by an alteration in a different variable. When statistics are used for this type of purpose they are known as **inferential statistics**. It can sometimes happen in research that two variables will appear to be connected, in the sense that as one varies the other will appear to vary as well. We might well suspect that there is a relationship here, but might be uncertain whether or not this is an apparent or real relationship. In such a case, statistics can be used to test the nature of such an apparent relationship. Such tests of **statistical significance** can help to determine the probability that relationships of this type are in fact real, or whether it is more likely they are due to chance or the effects of sampling.

Summary

When we are discussing the use of the scientific method in social research, it is helpful to appreciate that in its more general sense it embraces a logical, rational approach to enquiry, which is not restricted to methods which attempt to replicate the physical sciences. This chapter has attempted to link together a wide range of approaches to social enquiry, and to illustrate the factors they share. Although there are differences between qualitative and quantitative methods there are also features which link them, and the apparent ideological divide between these approaches to research is not as great as it may sometimes appear.

 **Further reading**

Dressman, M. (2008) *Using Social Theory in Educational Research.* Abingdon, Oxon: Routledge.

Field, A. and Hole, G. (2002) *How to Design and Report Experiments.* London: SAGE.

Gavin, H. (2008) *Understanding Research Methods and Statistics in Psychology.* London: SAGE.

Rugg, G. and Petre, M. (2006) *A Gentle Guide to Research Methods.* Maidenhead: Open University Press.

Saks, M. and Allsop, J. (eds) (2007) *Researching Health.* London: SAGE.

6

The Research
Design

Chapter objectives

This chapter will help you to:

- Understand different perspectives employed in writing about social science research.
- Consider issues of design and structure in research.
- Evaluate questions of data analysis in research.

Terms used

The following terms are discussed in this chapter: biographical research; case study; conversational analysis; correlation; criterion-referenced test; critical theory; ethnography; ethnomethodology; existentialism; expost facto research; feminist theory; focus group; hermeneutics; longitudinal study; meta-analysis; metanarrative; non-parametric test; norm-referenced test; oral history; oral narratives; parametric test; personal accounts; phenomenology; pilot study; stream of consciousness; symbolic interactionism; teacher-researcher.

Social science research perspectives

One of the features of social science research is that researchers will have at their disposal a wide range of different theoretical approaches or perspectives to draw upon for their research. Such perspectives are important because they provide a framework around which the research design may be constructed. In effect, they link together all aspects of the research process. Each separate perspective is usually associated with a specific type of data collection, and also with types of analysis. This enables the researcher to select a perspective which is appropriate and relevant for the aims of their research.

Ethnography is a popular research perspective, perhaps because it offers researchers a degree of flexibility, and the possibility of using a range of data types. Its broad approach is derived from social anthropology. The early anthropologists often travelled to distant cultures and countries, and lived within societies, usually for a sufficient length of time to learn the local customs and language. They attempted to look at the world through the eyes of the members of that society, and to understand the world as they did. They tried to make sense of the relationships within the community, of the way power and authority were distributed, and of the interaction between the genders. In short, they attempted to understand all aspects of the community they were studying.

Ethnographers have adopted this methodology but applied it to communities nearer home. They have typically studied within their own country different social groups, including groups of different ethnicity or religion, organizations or settings such as schools, colleges, housing estates and businesses, and occupational groupings or people living on the margins of society in some way. In other words, ethnographers will select their subject matter from a very wide range of contexts. The word 'ethnography' is used, on the one hand, to describe the broad methodology, while on the other hand, *an* ethnography is the written account derived from an ethnographic research study.

An ethnographic account tries to achieve a number of different objectives. One feature common to most ethnographic research, is that the researcher will try to adopt the viewpoint of those people who make up the social setting. The researcher does not pre-determine the nature of the research, but tries as far as possible to let the participants or social actors (as they are sometimes known in ethnographic studies) determine the key issues in the research. This can be contrasted with survey research within a positivist tradition, where the researcher designing a questionnaire normally determines the nature of the questions to be asked. In examining the social world as viewed by the participants or actors themselves, the ethnographer tries to understand the meanings which they attribute to events. One of the assumptions of ethnographic research is that people may look at the same social event in different ways depending upon their own perspective. In other words one person may view an event as having significance and meaning in their life, whereas for another person the same event may be regarded as insignificant. The ethnographer is interested in the functioning and evolution of the way in which meanings are attached to events, and in particular is interested in differences in perception between different communities and societies.

We often notice that institutions of the same type can differ enormously in their 'atmosphere' and 'tone' when we enter them. Think of the differences between high schools for example, or those between hospitals. They may receive approximately comparable resources and be located in comparable areas, yet be very different in nature and character. Ethnographers are interested in exploring the reasons for these differences. In constructing an ethnography of a school for example, the ethnographer would try perhaps to describe the nature of the relationships between the staff, and between the teaching staff and the school management. Having attempted to describe the nature of those relationships, the ethnographer would seek evidence and explanations for these relationships. Explanations might lie in the management style of the headteacher, or in the behaviour of the pupils, or in the structure of the school. In achieving these explanations, the ethnographer will utilize any kind of data available, from interviews and observational data, to collecting documents and keeping notes in a diary.

The research literature on ethnography is extensive, including both research studies which employ ethnography and also more theoretical discussions of the perspective. McNamara (2009) analysed the use of feminist ethnographic approaches in research in social work, while Vrasti (2008) evaluated the use of ethnography in researching international relations. Savage (2006) has explored the use of ethnographic data in research in health studies, a context in which it has often been particularly relevant. In addition, Lillis (2008) used an ethnographic perspective to study academic writing.

One of the initial issues for ethnographers is that of gaining access to the setting in which they will conduct their research. Almost inevitably this involves obtaining permission from people in authority and this may sometimes be withheld. An organization may simply not want someone collecting data on every aspect of its structure and function. Ethnographers will sometimes choose to collect data within an organization to which they already have access, for example the school or college where they teach. There are both advantages and disadvantages to such an arrangement. On the positive side the **teacher-researcher** will already be aware of the details of that organization, will know people there, and will also have access to most aspects of the daily life of the organization. In general it will probably be relatively easy to collect data, and presumably colleagues will help in giving interviews and providing other data. However, on the assumption that the headteacher or college principal is quite happy for the research to be conducted, there may still be practical limitations on the researcher. If the researcher teaches in the school, he or she may feel an implicit need to moderate any potential criticisms of the institution, simply because they have to maintain good relationships at their place of work. In effect, there may be practical limitations on the thoroughness with which the research can be conducted.

? — **Questions to consider**

Before obtaining permission to conduct research such as an ethnographic enquiry, it is worthwhile considering whether you will show the final research report to anyone for approval.

Will you simply disseminate the research report, and will you ask a key respondent, for example, to approve its accuracy?

A further complexity may also lie in the very fact that the researcher is so familiar with the social setting. When we work in an institution, and are able to see the way it functions on a daily basis, we may take much of that organization for granted. We will tend to be familiar with the patterns of work of the staff, and the general sequence of life in the institution. It is therefore easy to overlook things which an external ethnographer might find very significant. Hence one of the problems for the teacher-researcher is to try to observe the setting as if they were completely new to it. This may often be difficult, and is but one dimension of the general problem of role conflict which faces teacher-researchers. In this position they have, on the one hand, to fulfil the requirements of their job, while on the other hand, they must maintain progress with their research. Inevitably, from time to time, there may be conflicts between these two roles.

Throughout the conduct of the research, an ethnographer will try to disturb the research context as little as possible. The adoption of such a naturalistic approach is not always easy, as it can be argued that the mere presence of the researcher transforms the research context to some extent. When someone new enters any social setting, people will inevitably enquire about the newcomer, and depending upon the circumstances may change their behaviour considerably. This will certainly be the case if the newcomer is perceived in any sense as being someone in a position of authority. Even in the case of a teacher-researcher, there will almost certainly be changes in the context of the school or college. For ethical reasons, a researcher would need to disclose to his or her colleagues the fact that he or she was conducting an ethnographic study. We can imagine then, that as the researcher sits in the staffroom having a chat to colleagues, they would inevitably be wondering whether this was a social discussion or whether in fact the researcher was thinking about collecting data.

In ethnographic research, as in other forms of research, decisions have to be taken about the people who will be approached to provide data. It is not normal in ethnography to seek a probability sample, as it is rarely the case that a researcher is intending to attempt any statistical generalization. Nonprobability or purposive samples will normally be sought, although it is still important that the researcher has a clear and justifiable sampling strategy. In most ethnographic studies, important criteria in the selection of respondents are whether they have the kind of specialist knowledge of the research setting which will enable them to provide interesting data, and secondly, whether they are willing to devote their personal time to providing data. The latter is a not inconsiderable issue, since participation in an ethnographic study can be very time-consuming for those who choose to provide data. Besides these basic considerations however, it is important that the ethnographer tries, for example, to identify respondents from different social or other categories within an organization, or attempts to find respondents who are representative of different roles. Even though this selection may not reflect a statistical representation, it is still important that the sample is sufficiently diverse to enable some kind of cross-checking of the data. Such triangulation can be very important in ethnographic studies, as it enables researchers to check the validity of the data provided.

One further aspect of ethnographic research is the issue of cultural or other differences between the researcher and the community he or she is studying. The argument here is that if there are differences in world view between the researcher and respondents, it may be more difficult for the researcher to view the world through the eyes of the respondents. These differences might be many and varied, including gender, ethnicity, religious background, political differences, social status, power differentials at work, or age. This is not to say that any of these factors may provide an automatic or necessary obstacle to establishing a rapport with respondents, or indeed in understanding their perspective on the world. Yet it is always worth the researcher being aware of the potential effects of such factors in providing limitations to understanding. Thus it is not to say that a person of one religion could not conduct an ethnographic study on a group from another religion, but merely to be aware of at least the potential for misunderstandings based on different perceptions of a situation. It might be perfectly possible for an older researcher to conduct ethnographic research on teenage rock bands, particularly if that researcher has some specialist knowledge of the field or of the vernacular of young people. Depending upon the individuals concerned however, there may be issues with establishing empathy and gaining access and acceptance within the research field. A further example might be where there are significant power or status differentials between a researcher and the people acting as respondents in a workplace. Such differences in status may not necessarily prove to be a problem, but there is the possibility at least that they may make communication somewhat difficult, and might also affect the way in which the researcher interprets the data. In short then, while researchers should not feel that such differences are an obstacle to the planned research, it is probably sensible to be aware of their potential effects, and to try to minimize these wherever possible.

It is usually helpful for the readers of research studies to appreciate the specific orientation of the ethnographer who has conducted a particular study. For example, if a researcher is a committed member of a political party, and shares that specific political ideology, this may in some implicit fashion affect the way in which he or she collects and analyses the ethnographic data. This type of research very much concerns the interpretation of data, and hence our own view of the world will almost inevitably affect the manner in which we attribute meaning to things. In order therefore not to cause any confusion, and also because of a desire for open and honest research, ethnographers will sometimes write accounts of their own academic background and the belief systems to which they subscribe, and attach these to the account of their research, perhaps as an appendix. This type of account is often known as a reflexive account. The reader of the research report or thesis is thus able to appreciate the particular perspective with which the researcher has approached the question or issue under investigation.

A second perspective very much connected with ethnography, and sharing some its basic approaches, is **symbolic interactionism**. A popular approach in sociology and social science research, this perspective emphasizes the manner in which human beings interact to create shared meanings. Reality is not seen as fixed or pre-determined, but as literally created between human beings. When one person expresses an opinion about something and another person responds, they are in the early stages of negotiating a sense of shared understanding about the world. As they continue to share their thoughts and feelings, they will either reach a consensus and realize that they share a common viewpoint or they will agree to differ. Along the way they will probably influence each other's thinking considerably. This interaction will inevitably proceed through the use of symbols. Words themselves are the clearest examples of symbols. Words are not reality themselves, but they do represent or symbolize reality. So, for example, the word 'table' is not actually a table, but it *stands for* or symbolizes a table. When we come across this symbol, orally or in writing, we know what it *means*. Words, however, are not the only symbols. The media, and particularly television, use an almost infinitely large number of symbols. However, symbols can be very ordinary objects. When we meet someone for the first time, we might offer them a cup of tea or a drink. This is not exclusively because we feel they have a physiological need to take in liquid; the offer is of course a symbol, an offer of openness, of a willingness to talk and discuss things, and a gesture of friendliness. Hence symbolic interactionism is the study of such symbols, and the way in which we use them in our exchanges with other human beings.

It is not always easy of course for researchers to identify the meaning and significance of the symbols used in interactions. They need to collect very detailed observational data, including details of spoken exchanges, in order to be able to analyse the creation of meaning between two individuals. The workplace is a typical arena in which meanings are continually being defined and re-defined. In a committee meeting, for example, someone may feel that an issue is very important and will thus open up the possibility of a debate on that issue. The chair of the meeting, or perhaps some others present, may either by their attitude or what they say indicate that they do not feel the issue is very significant. That may cause the first individual to revise his or her opinion, and to drop the issue. On the other hand, it may reinforce their determination to pursue it. However, any discussion or verbal exchanges will contribute to the way in which the different social actors view the situation.

A central pillar of the perspective of symbolic interactionism is that there are many different and legitimate ways of viewing the social world. The latter is seen as being in a state of constant flux. Ideas and concepts are being exchanged between individuals at all times, and people's perceptions of the world are being altered by these interactions. There does not appear to symbolic interactionists, to be anything fixed or definite about the social world. If everyone is continually negotiating new understandings about the world, then it follows that there will be many different perceptions and meanings attached to the same object or idea. In other words, people will reflect multiple perspectives about the world.

For the symbolic interactionist researcher, the key perspective is to accept the vision of the world as perceived by the research respondents. The world exists as the social actors perceive it. There is, from this viewpoint, no purpose in the researcher presenting the world in a certain way, if the respondents view it completely differently. Very often therefore, researchers will find themselves presenting unconventional, alternative, and unorthodox views which are often in contrast to the accepted and conventional views of society. In the case of, say, an interactionist study of homeless people, one can easily imagine that their view of society will be rather different from that of people fortunate enough to have a secure income and somewhere to live. Within the confines of the study, reality for the interactionist will be defined by the views of the homeless people themselves. If they view the institutions of society as being uncaring, unhelpful, and insensitive to their plight, then within the parameters of the research that is the viewpoint which is significant.

? ── **Questions to consider** ──────────

In the context of an interactionist study, it is important to try to look at the world from the perspectives of others, and to ask oneself:

Can I suspend my own vision of the world, and look at it through the eyes of my respondents?

Closely-related to symbolic interactionism is the perspective of **phenomenology**. This was originally developed as a philosophical orientation by Edmund Husserl (1859–1938), but has gradually become used in addition as a social science research perspective. It has also had a considerable influence on other interpretive approaches. Phenomenologists generally adopt the viewpoint that objects and events in the social world do not possess an intrinsic meaning. In other words, there is no absolute meaning or significance which attaches to an object. Meaning as such is derived from human consciousness alone. A mountain, for example, is just a mountain – a fold in the earth's crust composed of rocks, earth, and sedimentary deposits. That is all it is. However, if it happens to be Mount Fuji in Japan, then it is a spiritual object of reverence. For others a mountain might be a defensive barrier against invaders. For yet others, it may be a hunting ground or a place for sport or skiing. Thus for phenomenologists the world is full of meaning, but only because human beings will apply their minds and consciousness to an interpretation of the world. This tendency to employ our minds in attaching meaning to the world is known as intentionality. Phenomenologists suggest that we have a tendency to do this as part of a desire to understand our surroundings.

We are all of course affected by the process of socialization, whereby we are influenced in our understanding of the world through processes such as our upbringing and our education. Through socialization we will tend to absorb our understandings of the world from others. When conducting phenomenological research it is suggested that we suspend our attachment to these socialized beliefs and meanings, and try to look at the world with an uncluttered mind.

This, of course, is not always easy to accomplish. As we grow up we are continually influenced, directly and indirectly, by our families, teachers, and in a more general way, by the prevalent ideology of society – the composite of the beliefs and values which hold sway in the world around us. In the 1920s and 1930s, a group of intellectuals working at the Institute for Social Research in Frankfurt argued strongly that we are all affected by the predominant philosophy of capitalism. Of these thinkers Herbert Marcuse, who died in 1979, was probably the best known figure, and this group of academics as a whole became known as the Frankfurt School.

Their analysis of society was that contemporary society had become more and more dependent upon science and technology. Perhaps more than that, there had also arisen a form of psychological dependence upon science, such that people had an implicit faith in the possibility of scientific progress and the benefits that this would bring. The advance of science was also perceived as being linked to the advance of capitalist economic theory, so that the two became mutually dependent. A capitalist economy provided the necessary finance to fund the advance of technology. The latter, in its turn, generated wealth which contributed to further economic growth. The academics of the Frankfurt School adopted the name **Critical Theory** for their particular analysis of society.

The analysts of the Frankfurt School went further however in not only emphasizing the power of science, and the influence of capitalism, but also in asserting that the latter had managed to extinguish all opposition to its ideals of the market and free trade. The traditional critics of capitalism would have been the working class, arguing for more state intervention in society and the collaborative use of society's resources. The Frankfurt School argued, however, that the working classes had been in effect persuaded of the advantages of capitalism, by virtue of the many economic advances they had obtained. The end result was that the capitalism system held sway unchallenged by a different ideology, and that a free market philosophy linked to a technocratic society became the dominant world view.

Moreover, they felt that people were being lulled into accepting this situation. Capitalism exerted extensive control over people through the medium of consumer goods, a more affluent lifestyle, and the superficial benefits which seemed to accrue from the advance of technology. Nevertheless they felt that, in a philosophical and spiritual sense, human beings were the worse for this. They were somehow being dehumanized by this world view, and in a subtle way their freedom of action was being limited by capitalism. Although critical theory did not generate a specific methodology of research, in terms of particular ways of designing research projects, it nevertheless inspired an approach which sought to reveal the ways in which human beings respond, react, and exist in a society dominated by capitalist forces, and in which people try to exert their own humanity and individualism.

The latter idea is very similar to a central notion of **existentialism**. The philosophy of existentialism arguably originated with the Danish philosopher Kierkegaard, but is often associated with the French philosopher Jean-Paul Sartre. One of Sartre's key ideas is often expressed in the short proposition 'existence precedes essence', and it is this proposition that is often used to assert the humanity and individualism of people. Sartre argued that human beings are first created and born, and only after that are they able to determine the nature of their lives. This challenges a traditional notion of determinism – that our futures are in some way strongly determined by either genetic inheritance or by the forces of society. According to Sartre we, and we alone, are the determinants of the nature of our existence. This is, in other words, a clear supporting statement for the principles of free will and of self-determination.

Points to consider

Despite the term 'existentialism', this philosophical approach emphasizes not the fact of existence but what we choose to do with our existence. In other words, the emphasis is not upon life per se but upon the moral choices we make, and the direction in which we try to take our life.

Nevertheless, Sartre argued, this idea brings with it heavy responsibilities. First of all, within this framework it is not possible for people to lay blame externally for what happens to them in life. The assumption of existentialism is that we are all accountable for our own lives as they unfold. Although we are free to take whatever action we see fit, that very freedom brings responsibilities. We must accept the responsibility and consequences of our own freedom. On the other hand, this freedom opens up enormous potential for each and every one of us. This freedom enables us to have control over our own lives, and at the same time to take ethical decisions with that freedom. For Sartre it is important to lead an *authentic* existence. The reality of freedom places an existential requirement upon us to define the nature of our own existence. When we lead our lives in accord with this definition we are then living the authentic life. If, however, we lapse into simply living according to accepted social norms and conventions, then this is inauthentic.

Existentialists view the world as being fundamentally and intrinsically meaningless. This is related to the concept of giving meaning to our own lives. Just as we use our freedom to make sense of our lives, and to give meaning to our own existence, we also have the capacity to do this to the world. Objects and events in the world have a meaning, to the degree that human beings will allocate those meanings. There is much here that existentialism shares with phenomenology and with interactionism. Existentialists will sometimes refer to the intrinsic lack of meaning in the world as the absurdity of the world. This absurdity is also a source of anxiety, as human beings realize they need to act on the world to allocate meaning. Existentialism per se has not initiated a great many research studies, but it has pointed the way to research which trys to explore the way in which human beings seek to define for themselves the way in which they will live.

This attribution of meaning is also significant in research conducted within the parameters of **feminist theory**. Simone de Beauvoir, the French feminist and existentialist, and colleague of Sartre's, was well-known for her proposition that the role and nature of women is not something given at birth, or a quality that exists in an absolute sense. Rather it is a product of a social conditioning process, which creates for women a role which is defined as acceptable by society. Women are able, in an existentialist way, to redefine this role, and adapt their lives in whichever direction they see fit. Feminism has been particularly influential in defining new approaches to social science research. It has achieved this in two main areas – first in the content and subject matter of research, and secondly in the methodology used.

Feminist research has tried to draw attention to some areas of study which have perhaps been overlooked in the past, and not seen as particularly significant by male researchers. These include areas such as women's careers and the limitations placed upon them by either the need to bring up children, or indeed by the expectation that they would be the partner who would adopt the prime role in child rearing. A related area in relation to women's careers has been the male domination of many career areas, and indeed the over-representation of men in positions of responsibility. Another area is the way in which the social patterns of men may make it difficult for women to progress in careers, simply because they cannot participate in the types of social networking adopted by men. In short, the subject matter of feminist research is any area which is significant to women and is defined as important by women. There is also the significant issue that feminist research is not simply a question of the intellectual investigation of a question, but of trying to transform the world. In that sense feminist research has a political agenda, in that it not only wants to highlight inequalities and injustice, but also seeks to change the situation for the better.

Points to consider

The idea of using research as an agency of change is an interesting development and applies also, for example, to action research. Research is thus not seen as purely objective and disinterested enquiry, but as having a specific intention to initiate social change.

There has also been considerable debate about the methodologies used in feminist research. Some would argue, for example, that positivist methodologies are inherently masculinist in nature, as male researchers are said to have a closer affinity with data in a numerical form. However, there is an argument that survey research and statistical data have the capacity to summarize trends in society – about, for example, women in managerial positions – which are very useful for feminists in arguing about the nature of society. Indeed it could be argued that women will be the best people to be designing such research, as they will be better able to define the key questions to be asked. This is an issue which may also apply in some qualitative studies, where a male researcher may not be the best person to conduct a study. A female researcher may be better able to ask the kind of questions which are significant to the respondents, and to express questions in the type of language which is sympathetic to those providing data.

The nature of language is central to another important perspective in social research, that of **ethnomethodology**. Most of the different interpretive perspectives used in social research are interested in summarizing and providing an accurate description of the ways in which people act in the world, and make sense of the world. Concepts such as 'status', 'power', and 'authority' are employed to make sense of the social processes operating in the world. For example, when a teacher assesses a student assignment, the grade given is usually checked or moderated by either a colleague from the same institution or an 'external' person from a different institution. This helps to assure a consistency of assessment, and a comparability of standards between institutions. Sometimes, during this process, there will be disagreements between assessors. One person may think the original grade was appropriate; others might feel it was too high or too low. A discussion will then ensue, and in some cases the grade may be changed. During that discussion, it may be that one or other of the people involved will be able to exercise considerable influence over the outcome, because of their actual or perceived status or authority. What is of interest to the ethnomethodologist is not only that such a process of negotiation actually takes place, but also the mechanism by which it takes place.

The actual process primarily involves language, and for this reason the main method of research employed in ethnomethodology is that of **conversational analysis**. A researcher will usually make tape recordings of the discussions taking place between people (in this case the examiners and moderators), and then analyse carefully the kind of language used by people to express, emphasize, or impose their viewpoints. This method of research is thus interested in the minutiae of social interaction, and in particular in the linguistic processes which are usually at the heart of the way in which social agreements are reached between people. Ethnomethodology is thus concerned with a fundamental process at the heart of social interaction, but one which requires a very detailed analysis, at a micro level, of human discourse. An approach which does not quite operate at such a level of detail, but is still concerned with specificity, is the **case study**.

Many different types of research designs could, in a sense, count as a case study. In terms of definition much hinges on what we choose to term a 'case'. A case study does imply the idea of a single example as the object of a study. For example, a single person might be taken as a case study. Alternatively, one might consider a single institution such as a school or college, or perhaps even an administrative sub-division of an institution, such as a department or faculty. A case study could also involve a larger unit, such as a local authority, state, or county.

However, whether the case study is an individual person, a group of people such as a team, or an institution, or a geographical area, there are some general features of a case study which more or less apply to all situations. A case study should first of all have some distinctive features which will render it significant to study. Thus an individual person who is selected should have had some particular life experience or achievement which makes it especially worthwhile to collect data from them. Similarly, an organization that is chosen should be distinctive in some way. However, besides having distinctive or particularly interesting features, a case study should also provide data which in some way reflect the situation in other analogous cases. In other words, the case study should also ideally reflect some typical features which mean that a degree of generalizability can be undertaken. The ideal case study should thus have both some distinctive and unique features, but also some characteristics which are typical of other situations.

Points to consider

With regard to the term 'case study', we can appreciate some of the difficulties and overlap which will occur with social research terminology. In a sense an ethnographic study could very often be described as a case study. Distinctions between research terms are often difficult to define, and hence the importance for researchers to try to specify as clearly as possible the way in which they are employing concepts.

Issues of design and structure

Increasingly a good deal of research is being conducted by professionals in their own working environments. This is particularly true of educational research, where a teacher or lecturer will be admirably placed to collect data, often from their own students. However, this type of research is not without its problems, in particular in relation to the potential for role conflict. If a teacher, for example, is interviewing his or her own students for a research study, then those students will inevitably view the teacher as a 'teacher', and not as a 'researcher'. They will perceive the teacher probably as an authority figure. This may affect the way in which the interview proceeds, in the sense that it is likely to be less of a conversation between equals and much more a case of each respondent trying to answer questions. There is also the potential threat to validity – that the students will perhaps try to provide the response which they think the teacher wants, rather than saying what they truly believe to be the case.

Depending upon the subject matter of the research, there are also potential difficulties of role conflict with other professional colleagues. They may be uncertain on different occasions whether their colleague is acting as researcher and collecting data, or whether the teacher role is carrying precedence.

Some types of research can be appropriate for the teacher researcher, perhaps where they can be quite open about the nature of the activity they are undertaking. An example would be in **oral history** research, sometimes alternatively termed **biographical research**. Oral history might be thought of as a variant of case-study research. Certainly it requires the active and sympathetic collaboration of at least one respondent, and this may not necessarily be easy to obtain. An oral history research design might involve the collection of data individually from a number of different respondents, while maintaining the philosophical approach of aiming for detailed, rich data.

Oral history or life history approaches have been used in educational research, for example, to document the careers of teachers and to explore the social and other forces which have been influential in their lives as teachers. There are certain methodological facets of oral history research which are important. A respondent will inevitably select those aspects of their life which they would like analysed and documented. This selectivity is something which the researcher should be aware of, and particularly when the analysis of the data is conducted. Some respondents will be understandably cautious about providing their life history data, and it behoves the researcher to be very clear about how the resulting data will be used, and whether or how these will be published. It is clearly important here that respondents are fully aware of all aspects of the research before agreeing to take part. **Oral narratives** and **personal accounts** are terms which are also used to describe similar types of research. Before leaving this type of data it is worth mentioning the term **stream of consciousness**. Normally employed in literary autobiography, or at least work which is largely autobiographical in character, this approach enables the writer or first-person character of the work to disclose their thoughts as they are thinking them. Such a flow of thought can be difficult to read at times, but is intended to reveal something of the workings of the mental process. This has not been explored very much as a research methodology, but offers some potential. Among the many writers who have experimented in this way are Marcel Proust, Samuel Beckett, and James Joyce.

In the case of such qualitative, reflective data, there is usually a great deal of analysis to be done in terms of exploring the meaning inherent in those data. **Hermeneutics** is the study of the interpretation of not only written material, but also of other sources of information transmission. One key issue for hermeneutics is the question of who will ultimately determine the meaning of a piece of writing or data. For example, if we consider autobiographical data we might feel that, irrespective of what others feel, the ultimate meaning will be determined by the author. On the other hand, one might argue that a personal account may affect different people in different ways, and hence that there is some legitimacy to the argument that it is the reader who will determine the meaning. As has been discussed, the range of different approaches within interpretive social science are to some extent linked together by the notion that the researcher is trying to understand the way in which the respondent makes sense of the world, and attaches meaning to sur-rounding phenomena. In much of human communication there is a continual attempt to interpret the utterances or writing of other human beings, and this points to the central importance of hermeneutics.

A considerable number of the theoretical perspectives discussed so far are, to varying degrees, attempts to understand the world in terms of an overar-ching and comprehensive scheme of thought. Such attempts to embrace a large part of human understanding within a single scheme are sometimes known as **metanarratives**. On one level such grand schemes of thought can be very attractive since they appear to provide us with a single, simple, explanatory vision of the social world. With a metanarrative, we do not have to look elsewhere for alternative explanations. Marxism, for example, pro-vides us with an all-embracing economic, political and historical system which explains the nature of contemporary society, and predicts the way in which our society will develop. As such it could be described as a metanarra-tive. However, such explanations have been criticized because of the very comprehensive nature of their explanations. Their critics have argued that metanarratives tend to ignore the diversity of society and the consequent need to provide a variety of explanations. Society and social life, it could be argued, are so varied that no one explanation could ever be sufficient to under-stand and explain them. It is for this very reason that many researchers will decide to adopt a range of different research methods, in order to have the advantage of exploring an issue from different perspectives.

Questions to consider

If you intend to adopt a metanarrative within your research, it is perhaps wise to consider the following issues:

- What are the limitations of this particular world view?
- To what extent am I confident that it can be used to explain all the features of my research?

When designing a research study, it is therefore often useful to conduct a short, preliminary study in order to examine different potential ways of carrying out that research. Such a preliminary study is termed a **pilot study**. Such studies are often used to evaluate a draft questionnaire or interview schedule, in order to refine their structure. They may also be used to explore the way potential respondents react to a study, or to enable a researcher to practise the techniques they intend to be employed in the actual research.

Sometimes **focus groups** can also be used for this purpose, or as a data collection method in their own right. Focus groups can be a very useful alternative method to the interview. A small group of respondents will be assembled, and with the researcher usually acting as the chair person for the group a discussion will be initiated on the topic being researched. The researcher will usually try to ensure that the discussion remains within the broad scope of the subject, and will, from time to time, probably ask some relevant questions about the topic. One of the advantages is that a focus group can often develop its own dynamics, and will explore an issue with the minimum of intervention from a researcher. In such a case, there may be a number of interesting outcomes from that discussion, including perhaps some completely unanticipated outcomes. The group members may stimulate each other in terms of input to the discussion, and generate a range of ideas which the researcher may not have considered. On the other hand, there is usually not the same opportunity to ask in-depth questions of individuals in the same way as with a one-to-one interview. Nevertheless, there are practical advantages to being able to collect data from a group of people in much less time than would be the case with one-to-one interviews. In addition, and as noted above, focus groups can provide a useful forum within which an outline research design can be discussed and evaluated by potential respondents.

There are, however, other forms of research design which can prove useful within certain research contexts. As a general rule, empirical research involves collecting data concerning events which are happening now, in the present, or events which might happen in the future, for example, through conducting experiments. In the latter case the interaction of variables is studied, to try to determine how one variable may affect the other. In some cases, however, an event may have already occurred and we are now interested in trying to analyse the causal factors for that event. In such a case we cannot reconstruct the actual event, and hence will have to look back at whatever evidence is still available which might suggest the origins of the situation.

For example, education managers may notice that there was a relatively high turnover of teaching staff during a two year period, and will wish to try to understand the reasons for this. The exact same circumstances would be unlikely to happen again, and thus it is not possible to investigate the situation as if it were happening at this moment. However, by looking back at the situation, and trying to collect as much data as possible in retrospect, researchers may be able to reconstruct the key factors which influenced the social situation. Resignation letters from teachers may still be on file; school principals may have recollections about discussions held with teachers; it might be possible to locate former teachers and enlist their help in providing interview data; and there may be student performance data from the period that could provide an indication of the general tone of the schools involved. Research of this type, where researchers look back at events in the past and attempt to reconstruct the causes of such events, is termed **ex post facto research**.

Other research designs will take a long-term view, but will do so by projecting forward into the future. **Longitudinal studies** will often take a group of respondents and study them over a prolonged period of time. The respondents will usually have been selected because they possess some factors in common. Such studies are useful for detecting long-term trends rather than simply collecting data during a short time period. There are, however, some difficulties with longitudinal studies, including the changes in extraneous variables during an extended period, and also the likelihood of some respondents withdrawing from the research during such an extended period.

Issues of analysis

An interesting range of terminology is used to describe different techniques of analysis used for the variety of research perspectives. In educational research pupil performance is sometimes measured and analysed via a number of different achievement tests. These can be divided into two types – **criterion-referenced tests** and **norm-referenced tests**. In the former type of test, a specific competence or ability is measured in pupils. For example, researchers might be interested in the capacity of primary school pupils to ensure that the subject of a sentence agrees with the verb being used, in terms of being singular or plural. This agreement is the criterion being tested. The researchers will generally be interested in the number of pupils who can demonstrate this competence.

On the other hand, a norm-referenced test is often used to compare different pupils. Researchers would therefore probably ask themselves the identity of the pupil who was apparently the most efficient at the task. They would then try to rank-order the pupils in terms of how well they accomplished the task. The essential purpose of norm-referencing is to list respondents in the order in which they have demonstrated competence in the particular field in question.

Variables in research can be compared in a variety of ways. In **correlation** or correlational studies an evaluation is made of the extent to which one variable varies with another. If as one variable increases the other increases approximately in proportion, then the correlation is termed a positive one. On the other hand, if one variable diminishes in value when the other increases, then the correlation is regarded as negative. A correlation between two variables indicates the presence of a 'relationship' or that the variables are connected in some way. However, it does not indicate that one variable is causing the other to change. There may be a range of other factors which are influencing the variables and causing them to change in the way that they do. To put this in a succinct way, correlation is not necessarily causality.

Statistical tests of significance can be used to estimate the possibility of a relationship between variables. These tests are sometimes divided into **parametric tests** and **non-parametric tests**. The former make the assumption that the data are obtained from populations which are normally distributed and have a similar variance. They also assume that the data are measured using a scale of equal intervals, as is the case for example with a scale measuring temperature. These requirements for a parametric test are termed 'parameters'. Non-parametric tests do not have such requirements.

Finally, an interesting type of analysis that is sometimes used in social science research is **meta-analysis**. In this technique researchers will select a group of research articles or reports and re-analyse the findings. They will do this in hopes of identifying large-scale trends which have remained obscured in the individual studies.

Summary

Research design is a complex and sophisticated process. It is necessary first of all to have a clear idea about the aims of the research, and also about the theoretical perspective which will inform and underpin the totality of the research process. Methods of data collection and analysis will need to be selected to reflect the broad purpose of the research. This chapter has surveyed the issue of research design, and how this is connected with the different research perspectives normally employed in education and social science research. The ultimate purpose here is to create a thesis or a research report which has internal coherence, and where the aims at the beginning of the report relate to each main aspect of the research and also to the findings at the very end.

 **Further reading**

Davies, B. and Gannon, S. (eds) (2006) *Doing Collective Biography.* Maidenhead: Open University Press.

Gobo, G. (2008) *Doing Ethnography.* London: SAGE.

Huff, A.S. (2008) *Designing Research for Publication.* London: SAGE.

Krueger, R.A. and Casey, M.A. (2008) *Focus Groups: A Practical Guide for Applied Research* (4th edn). London: SAGE.

O'Leary, Z. (2007) *The Social Science Jargon Buster.* London: SAGE.

Ridley, D. (2008) *The Literature Review.* London: SAGE.

7

Data Collection Methods

 Chapter objectives

This chapter will help you to:

- Understand methods of data collection in the social sciences.
- Examine the terminology used to discuss data collection methods.
- Familiarize yourself with methods of data analysis.

→ **Terms used**

The following terms are discussed in this chapter: accounts; bias; biography; closed question; coding; content analysis; covert observation; data collection instrument; documents; fieldwork; gatekeeper; inference; insider; internet-based survey; interviews; key informant; multiple choice question; multiple perspectives; narrative account; nominal data; null hypothesis; open question; outsider; participant observation; participants; postal questionnaire; questionnaire; rating scale; reactivity; reflexivity; respondents; simulation; subjects; telephone survey; theoretical sampling; transcription.

Methods of data collection

On a philosophical level, the way in which researchers will collect data is connected to their approach to ontological and epistemological questions; in other words, to their overall view of the nature of reality, and to their idea of what should count as valid knowledge. Sometimes also, the subject matter of the research project will be a determining factor in the choice of a method of data collection. If we are interested in examining an issue which involves deeper human feelings, and where the emotions involved are very complex, then we may decide that we require a method which is capable of collecting rich, detailed data. In such cases, we may decide to employ the methods usually associated with qualitative enquiry. One popular method used in such a context is **participant observation**.

The essence of this approach is that we will observe a particular social context while at the same time engaging to a certain extent with that situation. While collecting data, we will try to become a part of the social context. This immediately reveals practical and philosophical issues connected with the approach. Social situations are living, evolving entities in which individuals are continually interacting and changing the situation. Imagine an office, a restaurant, a sports club, or a hospital. These are all social contexts with their own complex range of human interactions. On every occasion when a stranger enters that situation, the social interactions will inevitably change. People may talk to the newcomer, trying to place them in the social context. They might try to make sense of their presence, and locate them in the social network of the situation. Researchers will inevitably have this type of impact, and ironically in a way, will change the very situation which they are trying to understand. It is very difficult then for an observer to be detached from a social situation. Observers have to accept that they will be, to varying degrees, part of the situation they are researching.

Nevertheless, the degree of participation may vary on a continuum from one of extensive participation to one of as little participation as possible. To some extent this will depend upon the way in which the researcher designs the investigation, but it can also depend upon the subject matter of the research. For example, in school-based research a researcher may decide to obtain, in consultation with the headteacher, an actual teaching role within the school. In other words, the researcher in effect becomes a member of staff, teaches pupils, marks work, and socializes with other teachers in the staffroom. At the other end of the continuum from the fairly full participation role, a researcher may simply call in at the school for a few hours each week and observe a class. Equally, there can be many different variations in between these two extremes.

In all forms of participant observation, there will be important questions about ethics and about acceptance by those people who are normally part of a social context. If one adopts a role of minimum participation, it is generally easier for people to understand a researcher's role. A researcher is clearly understood to be exactly that. There is little apparent ambiguity about the researcher's situation. Researchers can explain their role and their work to the teacher and pupils who are being observed, and generally they will be able understand this and within certain limitations continue with their normal routines. In a situation of relatively full participation however, researchers will be adopting at least two significant roles. They will be researchers, but also social members in their own right. The ethics of such a situation would normally demand that they reveal the nature of their research to, say, the other teachers. However, one can imagine that the other members of staff would sometimes wonder about when the researcher was acting as a researcher, and when they were acting as a teacher. For example, if a researcher were chatting to another teacher in the staffroom, that teacher might wonder whether they were providing data for the researcher or whether they were having a normal social interaction.

Questions to consider

Participant observation raises questions about the application of the principle of informed consent, and also about whether permission has genuinely been obtained to publish the research findings. If a researcher collects data from someone without that person realizing they are participants in a research project, then there are significant ethical issues with this. It is worth the researcher asking him or herself:

- Have all the people who have given me data also given me their full authorization that they are willing to be a research participant?
- Have all the participants mentioned in the research report given their permission for the findings to be circulated as a report or publication?

Generally, participant observers will try to collect data from a situation which has remained as natural as possible. They will make an effort to disturb the social setting as little as possible. One of the major ways in which they can try to achieve this is to provide a clear justification for their presence. For example, a researcher may explain that he or she is collecting data for their research degree at a local university. This would probably be accepted by most people as a justifiable reason for their presence. If the research context was any kind of workplace employees would probably not be too concerned by this, particularly if they had been reassured that the management of the organization were not directly involved in the planning of the research. On the other hand, if the justification for the research was in any sense a review of work practices, then the researcher would have to appreciate that they may not be fully accepted by employees. Here there may be a feeling that the research was at least partly concerned with worker evaluation.

Participant observation is a widely-used technique that lends itself to many different types of research context. Bowen (2002) used this approach to research customer satisfaction in the tourist industry and Ezeh (2003) employed it in an anthropological study, while Allan (2006) applied the method in a study of nursing.

All forms of observational research will raise profound ethical questions about the role of researchers. It is vital to bear in mind the responsibility of researchers towards those being observed, and to ensure that they are treated as human beings and not simply as sources of data. If a researcher did not reveal their identity, or the reason for their presence, to members of the social situation, then it may be difficult to find an ethical justification for this type of **covert observation**. Participant observation does always raise difficult issues in this regard, but it is essential to continually reflect upon the ethics of researchers' actions.

Data collected by participant observers may be of various kinds, but central to the approach is the field diary. Most observers will try to develop systematic ways in which they can record their field notes. Ultimately, the purpose of the research will be to develop a theory concerning the social setting, and hence one purpose of the field notes will be to try to note the roles and relationships in that setting. The researcher will try to establish the nature of formal and informal networks and relationships, the existence of lines of communication, the nature of power and status relations, and the social patterns of the setting. The researcher will also try to impose a form of theoretical understanding upon the social setting, and at the same time record any data and evidence to substantiate these understandings. These data will then be adduced later in order to justify the written accounts produced by the researcher.

Participant observation is one of the commonest data collection methods associated with ethnographic research. It very much lends itself to studies where researchers are seeking to understand a different culture, and also to understand a social context from the point of view of participants. In participant observation, just as in ethnographic research in its totality, the prevailing philosophy is one of trying to see the world through the eyes of others, rather than trying to impose on the social world the perceptions of researchers. The use of **interviews** as a research method can potentially provide a compromise between these two epistemologies. Interviews may be employed in a way which has a lot of similarities with a positivistic approach, while on the other hand they might be employed as part of, for example, an ethnographic study to examine the perspectives of social members.

An interview may be used, first of all, in a very formal way, perhaps as part of a survey. In this case, an interview schedule or proforma will be drawn up which may not appear to be very different from a questionnaire. This will have a range of pre-planned questions which the researcher will have designed in advance, and which reflect the issues which the interviewer feels are important in the study. In this sense, the formal or structured interview reflects a realist ontology. The researcher's perspective will be that there are clearly-defined realities which can be expressed within the scope of formal questions, and that the likely responses to these can be classified or categorized. The latter must be included in the interview schedule. After each question, the researcher will often list a range of categories of response. During the conduct of the interview, the interviewer will pose the questions one at a time, and then perhaps tick the category which best reflects the response. The data are then coded ready for analysis. Market research interviews are very often conducted in this way. The process will normally work smoothly if the responses fall neatly into one of the available categories. There will often be a general category to use if a response does not reflect one of the main divisions available. However, it is evident here that while a system such as this may be relatively quick to administer, it does not have the flexibility to accommodate variants of response or those which perhaps reflect a minority viewpoint. It is insufficiently adapted to being able to record the nuances of response which are often a feature of the way people think and feel.

Structured interviews also do not enable the interviewees to re-define the issues which they feel are important in an area. In a sense they have to accept the questions and concerns which have been determined by the researcher as being important. Often the researcher will have conducted a preliminary study in order to survey the issues which he or she would like to examine further. However, it is still the case that these are defined by the researcher. This approach, however, is well-adapted for use in **telephone surveys**. An interviewer can telephone potential respondents, and put the questions to them from the interview schedule. They may already have the schedule on a computer, and hence will be able to input the responses directly as these are given. This is also suitable for computer-based research, where the interview schedule can be emailed to respondents. The latter approach enables a great many potential respondents to be contacted with a minimum of effort.

Both the interview schedule and the questionnaire are examples of what may be described more generally as **data collection instruments**. The interview schedule will usually contain more information than simply the questions to be asked. It may include a reminder to the interviewer of the information to be given to potential interviewees before the commencement of the interview. Interviewees should be informed about the nature of the research and how the data will be used before they are asked whether or not they would like to take part in the research. The schedule may also include a reminder to the interviewer about things to be said on the conclusion of the interview. This may be a reminder about one or two formalities, such as thanking the interviewee for their time, and it might also include a brief restatement of the purpose of the research.

At the other extreme of the continuum of types of interview is the unstructured or informal interview. Ontologically-speaking this type of interview does not assume the existence of rigid, precise realities in the world, but rather that reality is continuously constructed within the minds of individuals. Therefore the purpose of research is to interpret the nature of this subjective reality, and to understand the distinctive perceptions of individual human beings. Hence the unstructured interview sets out to provide a vehicle whereby the interviewer can discuss and explore reality as seen through the eyes of the respondent. In the most informal variant of the unstructured interview the researcher will probably only determine the general nature of the subject to be discussed. The topic will be introduced to the respondent, and from then on the direction and tone of the interview will be largely determined by the interviewee. One advantage of this approach is that there may be unanticipated outcomes from such an interview. Although the interviewer may privately think that she or he has a clear idea of the prime issues in the research, it may well be that during the interview important new concerns may emerge of which the researcher was completely unaware.

This does not mean that the interview can be allowed to deviate completely off the subject. The interviewer will clearly have limits within which they must keep the discussion, but generally the way in which the discussion evolves will be left to a large extent to the interviewee. Between the two extremes described so far there is an almost infinite variety of possible interview formats, which will reflect differing degrees of structure on the one hand or of informality on the other. To some extent, researchers can adjust the interview approach to suit the subject matter of the research, the context, and the nature of the respondents. The research schedule may range from something resembling a questionnaire, to a simple list of topics to be addressed. At the very informal end of the continuum, there will probably be no need for a data collection instrument at all.

Points to consider

Very informal, unstructured interviews almost cease to be interviews – they become discussions, conversations, or reflections. The 'interviewer' also almost ceases to have a role, except perhaps as a listener and occasional prompter. The interviewer will try to keep the 'interview' within the bounds of the research aims, but frequently the purpose of the research will be in effect redefined by the respondent.

Several different methods may be used to record the outcomes of an interview. In the case of a structured interview, a researcher may feel that a form similar to a questionnaire is sufficient. However, certainly in an unstructured interview, or in an interview where there is any degree of discussion about issues, tape recording will generally be the preferred method. This has the advantage that it records precisely what is being said without any ambiguity. Video recording offers the additional advantage that it can record those gestures and facial expressions which may indicate additional nuances of meaning. However, it also requires more complex equipment and is generally more intrusive for the respondent. Not all respondents will feel happy about being tape recorded, and it is an important ethical principle that they should be asked specifically if they object to the use of a recorder. It is also possible to take written notes of interviews, but there are clearly major restrictions in the use of such a technique. Only the key issues can be noted, and memory limitations may significantly affect the validity of the accounts produced from such data.

When tape recordings are produced, it is normal to transcribe the recording in order that there is a written account of exactly what has been said. This, however, is not always as simple as it may seem. Even assuming that the recording can be correctly interpreted, the way in which we speak is often far from grammatical and straightforward. We will often hesitate when we are speaking, repeat ourselves, use colloquial expressions and abbreviations, and often articulate our feelings in a less than precise manner. All of this has, in some way, to be conveyed on paper. There are also the many intonations we use in speech. We will emphasize some words, speak loudly and more softly at times, and pause for emphasis. For this reason, some researchers will use a system of written codes to try to reflect these nuances of spoken speech. When transcribing, there are then often important decisions that must be taken about the level of detail which the researcher will try to replicate in the written record.

Interviews do not necessarily need to be conducted simply on a one-to-one basis. They can be carried out by the interviewer using small groups of two or three interviewees, or with larger groups of 10 or 12 respondents. The latter situation is often known as a focus group. Group interviews do not permit the same exploration of detail as is possible with one-to-one interviews, but there are a number of advantages. There are, first of all, advantages of logistics for the researcher in collecting data from more respondents in a given period of time. Perhaps more important however, is the opportunity for respondents to discuss and raise issues between themselves. The interview is not entirely reliant upon the interviewer to raise issues. Interviewees will react to what each other has said, and in their responses, will almost inevitably raise new issues. This may well lead to a more interesting and fruitful discussion.

An important methodological concern with interview research concerns the process of interaction between interviewers and their interviewees. Sometimes, in work-based research, there may be power or status differentials between the interviewer and interviewee. This may be particularly so where the researcher is employed in the same organization as the interviewee. If the interviewer occupies a higher-status role in the organization, it may not lead to a very relaxed situation for the interview, and thus the subsequent validity of the data may be compromised. The interview process will also become complex when cultural differences exist between interviewer and the interviewee. This might be particularly significant in research involving, say, multicultural education or religious differences between communities. It may well increase the validity of the data if the interviewer and interviewee come from the same religious or cultural background.

A method of data collection which is closely-related to that of interviews is the use of **accounts**, or what may be rather more specifically known as **narrative accounts**. People may not necessarily need to be interviewed in a formal manner in order to produce a description or account of some aspect of their lives. A common example would be the autobiography. Many of these now exist, and they can be a rich source of data. However, as research data there are a number of issues which should be considered. A published autobiography is normally written from the viewpoint of attracting a readership, and hence the author may be selective about both the content of the book and the manner in which events are presented. This is not to say that it cannot be used as research data, but that the process and reasons for producing the data should be borne in mind. On the other hand, some people will write autobiographies or diaries for entirely private consumption. This may make it more difficult to access these as research data, but if they do become available then they may constitute rather more valid data. However, at all times when using such data it is important for researchers to consider the process of production, and the motivation of the person producing the account. As there is no interviewer to prompt the person, and as they have a free rein to select those items which they wish to include in the account, this raises questions about that process of content selectivity.

The use of a **biography** as research data may refer to several different situations. On the one hand, it may refer to a situation where a researcher is using a variety of data sources, including interviews, documents, and third person accounts, in order to compile a biography of a person. In such a case, that biography may not be dissimilar to what might otherwise be described as a case study or perhaps as an ethnography. However, existing biographies can also be used as research data – although in such cases, a researcher much bear in mind the various levels of selectivity and motivation which have operated. The original compiler of the biography will have amassed their data from the subject of the research. The research subject will have been selective in what they decided to talk about, and from those data the biography writer will have selected the material they regarded as most relevant. Finally, the researcher using the biography will again make selections based upon their perceived relevance for his or her research. All of these stages in the research process can add a possible veneer of threats to validity.

Nowadays, however, we have access to many variants of narrative accounts that have been produced using a range of media. Television and radio documentaries can offer a rich range of material reflecting the accounts of peoples' lives, and in addition, a rapidly-increasing amount of material is being placed on the internet. Some of this will be visual material, while other material will exist as **documents**. Besides documents which directly reveal aspects of individuals' lives, there is a wide range of documents of various kinds which are useful for research, even though these constitute secondary data. Governments will produce a wide variety of statistical material, and commercial organizations will publish data on profitability and sales for example. Educational organizations will also produce a wide range of documents, some of these reflecting evaluation data on schools and colleges. In general, there is an increasing tendency for organizations of all types to produce documentary data, and these can be a valuable source of data for researchers.

Points to consider

When using documentary data it is important to ask oneself the reasons for creating the document and also for saving it. Documents are not created by accident, and the process by which they are created may be just as significant as data, as the content of the document.

Of all the data collection instruments used in social research, the **questionnaire** is probably the commonest. In its traditional form, this was usually termed a **postal questionnaire** as this was the usual method in which it was distributed. This is still to some extent the case, although it might equally nowadays be distributed as part of an **internet-based survey**. It could perhaps most accurately be termed a 'self-completion questionnaire', since this reflects the philosophy behind this particular type of data collection instrument. The potential advantages of the questionnaire are enormous. It can in principle be used to gather data from a large number of geographically-dispersed respondents, in a relatively inexpensive way. If carefully designed, the questionnaire lends itself to automated, computer-based analysis, which reduces the work of the researcher considerably. Computer-based statistical packages further reduce the time-consuming aspects of the research. However, these notable advantages are matched by corresponding disadvantages, or at least by aspects of questionnaire design which must be carefully controlled if the data are to be valid, reliable and useful.

Questions to consider

It is important to remember that statistical analysis packages such as SPSS are only as effective as the person using them. It is very easy to learn how to input data, and to get some kind of analysis from the package. However, the results may be meaningless unless the correct type of data was used with the correct statistical test. It is important when designing a questionnaire question to ask oneself:

- What kind of data will this question generate, and do I know of a suitable test to use with the data?
- Will I be able to interpret the results correctly when I see them?

The questions must relate precisely to the aims of the research, and to the variables being investigated. Unlike during an interview, there will be no opportunity to clarify further the issues of the research. The questionnaire will be distributed once, and thus there is only that one opportunity to collect the necessary data. Equally, during the design of the questionnaire it is important to give consideration to the method of analysis and to the statistical tests (if any) which will be used to analyse the questionnaire. The nature of the data must be suitable for the intended statistical procedures. All of this demands careful thought in the design stage of the questionnaire.

The fact that a questionnaire will be distributed to respondents in the absence of a researcher, means that the questions must be very clear and easily-understood. It will not be possible for respondents to ask for any clarification of these. Equally, the questions should be as precise as possible and there should be as close a correspondence as can be managed between the information the researcher is trying to gather and the meaning conveyed by the question to the respondent. If this is not the case then different respondents will interpret the questions in different ways. Moreover, as a researcher is not usually present during the completion of such a questionnaire, it is difficult to know how much thought has been devoted to the task by the respondent. Some people may rush the task, while others might reflect carefully upon it. In other cases, respondents may be that eager to finish the task that they will not tick the boxes they intend, or may in other ways, not represent their actual views. Overall the possibility of respondent error is quite considerable.

It is important to take care with question design that the questions are not biased in any way, or suggest a particular type of response to respondents. Questions need to be phrased in a clear and precise manner, in order that respondents will understand them. The type of language which is used can be important. People who design questionnaires may be professional researchers or academics, and familiar with using technical vocabulary. If such terms are included in questions, they may confuse respondents. Essentially, the language style of the questions should be familiar to the intended sample of respondents. It is sometimes very tempting to refer to more than one issue in a question, or in effect, to ask two separate questions within one. This can also be confusing for respondents, and may cause them to not complete the questionnaire. When offering alternative responses to a particular question, it is important that the different categories do not overlap in any way. For example, in a question about respondent age ranges, categories might be zero to twenty years, and then twenty years to forty years. Respondents who were twenty years old might then opt for either category, thereby reducing the validity of the results.

A major factor in trying to ensure a high completion and return rate for a questionnaire survey is the formatting and physical design of the questionnaire. It is always worth remembering that the completion of a questionnaire makes demands on a respondent's time, and everything possible should be done to assist them with completion and in making the experience as pleasant and as straightforward as possible. Respondents are also more likely to be kindly disposed to a questionnaire which is easy to read, and is attractive in terms of layout. It often helps if there is a succinct covering letter to accompany the questionnaire, which explains the purpose of the survey and how the data will be used. At the beginning of the questionnaire there should be an introduction which provides clear instructions for its completion. Respondents should be told how to indicate their responses to the questions, such as with a tick in a box or by circling one alternative response. At the end of the questionnaire there should be clear instructions on how to submit the completed questionnaire, and also a statement of thanks to the respondent. Most questionnaires will include a section where biographical data are asked of the respondent. These questions might relate to their age, number of years in an occupation, or perhaps training courses undertaken. It is important that only the data strictly necessary to the research are collected here, and that the questions do not ask for data which respondents may regard as too personal. Respondents can justifiably be very sensitive about giving out personal information, and an inappropriate question may deter them from completing the rest of the questionnaire.

A common type of question structure employed in a questionnaire is the **rating scale**. This enables researchers to measure such variables as respondent attitudes in relation to a subject, and to quantify such responses, employing the data later in statistical analysis. A number of different rating scale designs are available. One of the commonest is the Likert scale. This poses a statement on a particular subject, and then asks the respondent to decide whether they strongly agree with the proposition, whether they merely agree, are unsure, disagree, or strongly disagree. If an odd number of alternatives are provided, then it is possible to offer a middle choice for those respondents who are undecided. Likert scales with an even number of alternatives are also possible. The Semantic Differential scale asks respondents for their opinions or attitudes towards an issue. They are presented with a numerical scale with opposite descriptors at either end. These descriptors might be such terms as good/bad, enthusiastic/indifferent, or happy/sad. The respondent indicates, perhaps by circling a number, their perceived position on the scale between the two opposites. We now turn to examine a further range of terms which can be used in relation to data collection.

Terminology of data collection

In terms of data collection there is an interesting distinction between the different terms which are used to describe those people who provide data. Among those typically used are **subjects**, **respondents**, and **participants**. The word 'subject' tends to imply that the research process is being carried out *on* them, much as one might carry out an experiment on something or somebody. The term 'subject' carries, to some extent, a connotation of being rather passively involved in the research, and the researcher taking the initiative. It is therefore a term more typically used in positivistic research, and characteristically in experimental research. On the other hand, in interpretive research, where there is the assumption of more equality of status or importance between the researcher and those providing data, it is more common to find the use of a word such as 'participant'. This term tends to imply more of a shared involvement or responsibility for the research. However, throughout all genres of social science research the commonest term is perhaps that of 'respondent'. This is a more neutral term, simply implying a person who will respond to the demands of the research project. In interview research, the term 'interviewee' is often used to describe the person being interviewed. Occasionally one might find use of the term 'informant', to describe someone who will provide information on a subject within the research project. However, the latter term is much more commonly used in the expression **key informant**.

In ethnographic and participant observation research, the term 'key informant' is used to refer to an individual who possesses specialized knowledge of some aspects of research, and is thus able to provide data which would probably be unavailable from a different respondent. In interpretive research, the availability of possible key informants can sometimes determine the composition of a purposive sample. Ideally, the relatively small samples of interpretive research should be composed of as many key informants as possible, in order to generate the most detailed and informative data. It is often not possible to determine in advance whether someone will be a key informant. It is only after holding discussions with them, or collecting some preliminary data, that one would have an idea about the quality or depth of the data which they can provide.

When we are trying to gain access to any research situation in order to collect data, we will usually have to obtain permission to enter the research field from a person in authority. Such people are normally known as **gatekeepers**. While these people could normally be regarded as significant in terms of their authority in providing or not providing access to the research field, they can often be potential respondents in their own right. As they are often well-informed about the nature of the research field, they may also often be regarded as key informants or key respondents.

When we are collecting data in the research context where our respondents normally live their lives, then we will sometimes say that we are conducting **fieldwork**. However, this term is employed slightly differently in different subjects. In the biological sciences, for example, and also in such areas as geography and geology, practical data collection away from the laboratory is usually known as fieldwork. This might be in a marine environment in biology, or on a mountainside in geology. In anthropology, fieldwork tends to be used to describe data collection that taken place among the people or cultures one is studying, rather than academic work in a library or some other more theoretical context.

In education and social science research in general, fieldwork tends to describe the process of collecting data in a practical and everyday context, in contrast for example to the collection and analysis of secondary data in a library. In addition, the term 'field' describes the location in which the data are collected.

Points to consider

The term 'field' is also used in the sense of field research, where it may be practically synonymous with qualitative research. This can be rather confusing. The 'field' is really the place where data are collected. In a sense, if we were distributing questionnaires in a school or college we might legitimately claim to be doing fieldwork, even though the perspective might be positivistic in nature. 'Fieldwork' and 'field research' are thus terms whose meanings have really to be judged from the context in which the writer uses them.

The terms **insider** and **outsider** can sometimes be used in relation to field research. An insider in research terms is someone who is familiar with a particular research context, and perhaps knows the individuals who live or work there. If a teacher in a school decides to work part-time for a research degree, and collects their data in the school in which they work, then they can be classified as an insider. One of the difficulties of acting as an insider is that the setting is so familiar that the researcher may overlook some obvious features which nevertheless could be important in research terms. Aspects of student behaviour or of staff interaction may occur so regularly that they are easily overlooked. On the other hand, the major advantage is that a researcher does not have to spend a great deal of time in finding out about the research setting or identifying the key social actors.

An outsider, on the other hand, is someone who is a stranger to the research setting. A teacher conducting research in a different school to the one in which he or she teaches would normally count as an outsider. Certainly they would be familiar with many aspects of the job of teaching, and also with the teaching profession, but they would not know most of the details about the operation of the school, nor the staff members or students. The relative advantages and disadvantages are really the opposite of those detailed for insider research. A lack of awareness of the social setting is to some extent balanced here by the capacity to look at a context in a fresh manner.

Whether researchers are insiders or outsiders, they will inevitably interact with the social setting in which they find themselves. We cannot, as researchers, enter a setting without to some extent changing that setting, and also without, to some extent, being changed by it. We do not even need to say anything, as our very presence will change the way people behave. We can imagine an adult who is unknown to the students entering a college class and sitting quietly at the back of the room. It would probably only be a few seconds before one or two students would start to whisper, asking about the identity of the newcomer. They may think that the new person was there to observe them, or to observe the regular teacher. Certainly, however, their behaviour would be likely to change in a variety of ways.

We will often use the word **reactivity** to describe the phenomenon of the social behaviour of respondents changing because of the presence of a researcher. The respondents will 'react' to the presence of the researcher. Reactivity is thus a significant threat to the validity of the data. The respondents will no longer be behaving in their natural manner, and hence the data collected will reflect the impact of the researcher, rather than recording the situation in a naturalistic manner. Some researchers will try to collect data in such a way that the process does not have an impact upon the nature of the data. For example, the collection of documentary data as one walks through a building, or the collection of waste materials discarded at the back of a building (a process raising ethical issues), are sometimes suggested as non-reactive processes, or non-intrusive processes. However, it is arguable whether there is any form of social data collection procedure which does not produce at least some form of reactive response. The problem then becomes the way in which it is analysed in the written form of the research report.

The term **reflexivity** is also used to refer to this process of affecting the social setting, although the concept tends to embrace the two-way process of influence and interaction whereby both researcher and respondents (or research context) will interact with and affect each other. There are many ways in which a researcher can affect the respondents. The way in which questions are phrased; informal conversation between researcher and respondent; the choice of topics for the research; the personal style and body language of the researcher; and the degree of interest shown by the researcher in the everyday lives of respondents – all of these can have an impact upon the way in which respondents will view and respond to the research.

A further aspect of this phenomenon is that the way in which the researcher approaches the research (and the way in which the research is designed and carried out) is at least in part a feature of the background of the researcher. The decisions made by the researcher in terms of data collection may be influenced by the nature of his or her education in the past, or by the experience obtained in previous employment. In other words, researchers do not come to the research process like blank sheets of paper, but are accompanied by the education, training, and experiences of the past. These will condition, to at least some extent, the way in which they go about the data collection process. The researchers will also be affected in a continuous feedback loop by the research as it progresses, and by the contact and interaction with the respondents.

For these reasons, it has become relatively common practice for researchers, particularly in the ethnographic and participant observation fields, to write a short 'reflexive account' to be placed in the study as an appendix. This type of account may be only a few pages long, but will provide a kind of intellectual autobiography which will detail the key influences acting upon the development of the researcher. This enables the reader of the research report or thesis to appreciate something of the researcher's perspective when commencing, designing, and conducting the research. It provides an outline sketch of the principal academic perspectives of the researcher, and helps the reader to understand something of the nuances of the research account.

This is an important philosophical position to take, particularly in qualitative research, as it is a reminder that different researchers will have been educated in different intellectual traditions, and thus may approach an investigation of the same subject in a variety of different ways. In other words, one of the most important features of interpretive research is that researchers will possess **multiple perspectives**. They will look at the social world in different ways, and interpret it depending upon their own unique intellectual background. One might argue that this is just a slightly different way of looking at researcher **bias**. It is at least arguable that some form of bias is practically unavoidable in research. The subjective nature of interpretive research almost inevitably results in a particular orientation being taken towards research which we may term 'bias'. However, the advantage of the discussion of reflexivity is that it brings this out into the open, and in a sense, treats it as a means of enriching the research process rather than undermining it. The main requirement for the personal approach and dimension of the researcher to be viewed as an advantage is that it should be brought into the open and discussed in the public domain.

A very wide range of terms is used in the area of data collection. Some of these are specialist terms, tending to be used more or less exclusively within the field of research methods, while others have found their way into everyday usage. **Multiple-choice questions** in questionnaires are an example of the latter. Philosophically they would be associated with a positivistic approach, since they define for the respondent the range of possible responses. These can be used as the basis for quantitative and statistical analysis. Multiple-choice questions are an example of the more generic type of questionnaire question – the **closed question**. These are so called because the question does not permit any variation in response from the respondent, except perhaps if there is the possibility of the respondent writing their own alternative response if the alternatives do not provide the necessary choices. Questionnaires will sometimes, however, employ **open questions** which will pose an issue and then simply give the respondent space to outline their response. These then result in what are, in effect, qualitative data.

Points to consider

'Open' questions are open in the sense that a researcher will not attempt to predetermine possible responses in any way. If respondents can be encouraged to write detailed responses then open questions on questionnaires can be a very useful method of obtaining large quantities of qualitative data in a time-effective way. This can be much quicker than using interviews. However, the method does not provide the opportunity for interaction which will take place in an interview.

There is a range of terms which can describe the types of data which are generated by questionnaires. **Nominal data**, for example, are data which divide the sample of respondents into two or more named categories. For example, a question which asked teachers whether they taught a science subject or a humanities subject would divide these teachers into two nominal groups. This would not perhaps be a very precise question to ask, as it is formulated here, but it illustrates the point. The resulting data would be described as nominal data.

Sometimes a research design will not involve investigating a 'real' event, but will recreate in some way a social event. For example, a researcher might be interested in investigating a particular type of group teaching situation, and yet the exact model for this may not be available in the school or schools to which he or she has access. Therefore the researcher may decide to create an artificial situation which reflects the characteristics they are seeking. This could be described as a **simulation**, because it creates a model of a theoretical idea rather than taking a real, practical situation as the subject for the research.

Methods of analysis

The term 'analysis' is a difficult concept to discuss or define. Researchers will often speak of analysis they have carried out, but separating this from a mere description of the data is not always easy. In fact, analysis can achieve a variety of objectives. It can compare the data collected with data from similar or indeed, different situations; it can draw general themes out of the data, and enable us to make more general statements which will have wider applicability; it can take a range of isolated fragments of data and **infer** broader or underlying trends, which will can be useful for making predictions; and it can start us on the process of developing theories which can be useful to try to explain the reasons for the data taking the form they do.

In some forms of qualitative research, notably within the grounded theory approach, the sampling process is related to the process of data analysis. Using a grounded theory perspective, the first stage in the research process will be to collect some preliminary data, and to carry out an initial analysis. An attempt is then made to identify any themes or concepts which appear to emerge from the data, and these themes or concepts are thus examined in order to suggest a strategy for further data collection. The cycle then continues, with a progressive attempt to either identify new themes or amend existing ones. Gradually these themes will be fitted together into a social theory which will slowly develop more coherence and clarity. At each stage this developing theory will be used as the basis for determining the direction of the sampling strategy. In other words, the process of theorizing is inextricably linked to that of sampling. The name for this type of sampling process is **theoretical sampling**, and it is particularly associated with grounded theory.

Once the data have been collected, the first stage is often to change it into a form in which it can be analysed. Interview or focus group data, for example, are often in the form of tape recordings which will need to be transcribed prior to analysis. **Transcription** is a time-consuming process. In order to transcribe one short section of the tape, the latter will often have to be started and stopped several times. If you are typing the transcript directly into a computer, or even if you are handwriting it initially, this process can be speeded up by using a foot control attached to the tape recorder. This frees you to type continually or to write. Overall, it will take a disproportionate amount of time to transcribe a very short section of recording. However, the work can sometimes be reduced by eliminating at the transcription stage some of the routine exchanges which take place in any conversation.

There are, however, a number of other important issues with transcription. One of the most important is the level of detail which will be used. Recordings of interviews and discussions will include many other features than words alone. Sometimes an emphasis will be put on words or phrases; sometimes irony will be used to express humour; and there can be a variety of pauses and changes in tone and volume which may indicate a variety of issues among the speakers. The essential question is the extent to which these should be indicated in the transcript, and also the method which should be used. Researchers will very often implement a number of different diacritical marks to indicate such changes of emphasis. A question remains, however, as to the level of detail which one should include, and also the type of naming or numbering system which should be used in order to hide the identity of respondents.

Different types of research will require a different degree of detail in the transcription. Traditionally, ethnomethodology concerns itself with the very detailed analysis of small sections of transcribed text, and it is usually necessary to employ a range of symbols to indicate pauses in the dialogue, emphasis, or emotive discussion involving irony, for example. On the other hand, a great deal of interview research does not concern itself with such detailed analysis. Depending upon the type of analysis which is anticipated, it is advisable for researchers to determine in advance of transcription a range of symbols which can be used to indicate subtleties and nuances in the text. With regard to ensuring anonymity, a variety of numerical or alphabetic symbols can be adopted to replace the real names of respondents during transcription, although these do tend to give a rather artificial tone to the text. The alternative is to give fictional names to respondents, of the same gender, cultural or ethnic group, so that the new name maintains something of the identity of the original respondent.

During the analysis of transcribed data it will often be necessary to identify themes or significant terms, or to group terms together and give them an overall name. In other words, the process of analysis involves (at least partly) the identification of significant concepts in the data, which might ultimately be used to develop a social theory. This process is often termed **coding**. The same term is also used for the part of questionnaire analysis where numbers are attached to different alternatives in the questions, to assist with the quantitative analysis.

In some forms of qualitative data analysis, an attempt will be made to identify the most significant concepts in a text, or piece of qualitative data, and perhaps also to identify the number of different times a concept is used. This process can reveal the extent to which the respondent or writer is relying upon a particular concept in transmitting ideas. It is part of an overall analytic process known as **content analysis**. Having identified the key concepts, the next stage of the analytic process is to try to explore the relationships between these concepts. As noted earlier in distinguishing between induction and deduction, the process of qualitative analysis is often one of trying to develop social theory rather than testing it. In terms of the latter, one of the central conceptual processes is one of proposing a hypothesis about the world, and then testing it. The hypothesis is frequently expressed in the form of a **null hypothesis**. For example, in a study of potential differences between male and female students and their performance in learning a foreign language, one might start by proposing that there was no difference between the genders and then test this assertion. Having collected the data, and subjected these to a statistical test, we may conclude that on balance we are able to reject the null hypothesis, and suggest that the evidence appears to point to a significant difference between males and females. On the other hand, we may feel that the data and statistical analysis suggest that we cannot reject the null hypothesis, and so we can provisionally assume that there is no significant difference between males and females. The form of language to be used here is very important, since statistical analysis does not actually prove anything to be true. Rather it points to a level of probability. As with all social research, we should always try to remain aware of the provisional nature of the conclusions we draw, and be prepared to amend our conclusions in the light of new data.

Summary

This chapter has explored some of the vocabulary and terminology used to discuss the methods of data collection. The process of collecting data is at the very heart of research. Without a suitable range of data, collected from an appropriate sample, a research project will not come to a successful conclusion. It is the stage in the research process where all the writing of aims, and of designing the research, comes to fruition. It can also be a stage in the research where unanticipated practical problems will arise, and will have to be surmounted. This chapter has reviewed both methods of data collection, and the related terminology, and also the concepts used in the methods of analysis of the data.

 **Further reading**

Drew, C.J., Hardman, M.L. and Hosp, J.L. (2008) *Designing and Conducting Research in Education*. London: SAGE.

Freshwater, D. and Lees, J. (2009) *Practitioner Research in Healthcare*. London: SAGE.

Haslam, S.A. and McGarty, C. (2003) *Research Methods and Statistics in Psychology*. London: SAGE.

Johnson, B. and Christensen, L. (2008) *Educational Research* (3rd edn). London: SAGE.

MacLure, M. (2003) *Discourse in Educational and Social Research*. Maidenhead: Open University Press.

Padgett, D.K. (2008) *Qualitative Methods in Social Work Research* (2nd edn). London: SAGE.

8

Questions of Ethics

Chapter objectives

This chapter will help you to:

- Understand the range of terms and concepts used to discuss research ethics.
- Evaluate the ethical arguments employed in social science research.
- Analyse the data collection procedures designed to comply with ethical considerations.

Terms used

The following terms will be discussed in this chapter: absolutism; access; anonymity; beneficence; code of practice; confidentiality; covert research; dissemination; ethical contracts; human dignity; informed consent; non-maleficence; permission; privacy; relativism; remuneration; sensitive context; situation ethics; utilitarianism; value free; values.

Principles of research ethics

At its very heart the key principle of research ethics is that one ought to treat the people who help you with your research with care, consideration, and sensitivity. To use a different term, we might say that we should at all times respect the **human dignity** of those who help us. It is always worth keeping at the forefront of our minds that our activities as researchers could not continue if it were not for the many people who are prepared to provide us with background information, give us access to research contexts, and indeed provide us with valuable data. The latter people are of course particularly important to researchers. Without respondents, the research process could simply not continue.

The research process will usually be very important to the researcher, but much less so to the respondent. The latter may well find the subject interesting to some degree, but on the other hand they may not be interested at all. To take part in the research may be time consuming – and not a little inconvenient. Respondents may also be asked to think about things, or to discuss topics, which normally they might be a little reluctant to do. Such issues might be personal or sensitive to them, and in everyday circumstances they might prefer to avoid them. Respondents may also need to travel in order to take part in the research, and thereby incur a degree of expenditure. When we combine all of these concerns we should realize that we are not offering respondents a great deal when we ask them to take part in a research project. In fact we are asking them to give to us, rather than the opposite. In such circumstances, the very least we can be expected to do is to think carefully about the feelings of the respondents before, during, and after the process.

In terms of human dignity it is essential that we never forget that research respondents are, above all, human beings. It is easy for researchers in all subjects and areas to become so preoccupied with collecting their data that they forget about the dignity of the person providing these. One way in which researchers can give something back to respondents is to be aware of the ways in which that research might help them or other people. If we explain this to respondents, then it may give them a sense of fulfilment in taking part in the research. It is also useful for researchers to reflect continually upon ways in which research may help society and other human beings. Although it is possible to conduct research purely with a view to understanding the social world rather better, or of adding to the sum total of knowledge, it is also a useful **value** to try to conduct research which, in some way, helps other people.

Conducting research which has inherent values is also useful when we are **disseminating** research, as it is easier to justify what we are doing to others and perhaps to members of the public. Research does not exist in an isolated world where it is sufficient simply unto itself. Research exists in a social world, where non-academics will assist us in our work, and where they are entitled to know what we are doing and to question the values inherent in the way we work.

Of all the values which exist as part of the research process, one of the most important is **informed consent**. When we ask people to take part in a research project it is very important that we provide them with all relevant information, so that they can decide for themselves whether they would like to participate. It is essential that we do this in order to preserve the autonomy and independence of those who may become our respondents. It would not be fair to try to persuade people to take part, without giving them the kind of information upon which they could take a rational decision. To do otherwise would be to undermine their human dignity, and also in a real sense to exploit them.

A very practical question arises however with the principle of informed consent. A researcher will need to decide what it means to be 'informed', and hence which information about the research should be made available. As with many issues in research ethics, it is probably not possible to devise a very precise and all-encompassing check list, but certain general principles should be followed. Potential respondents should be aware of the nature of the research project and of its purposes. Respondents may or may not be able to understand all the complexities of a research project, but the key features of the research should be communicated in ways which they can understand. This may involve the use of non-technical vocabulary. In addition, potential respondents should be made aware of the type of data which it is intended to collect, and the way in which these data will be used. They need to be made aware if they will be asked questions on sensitive issues, about which they may wish to think carefully before responding. Sometimes researchers may intend to archive data for future use and analysis, and respondents should be made aware of any such intention. They need to be reassured that the data they provide will be disseminated in a completely anonymous fashion, and that every possible precaution will be taken to prevent a possible identification of respondents from information provided in a research report or thesis. Potential respondents will certainly want to understand the nature of the data collection process, in order that they can anticipate the type of experience they will have if they agree to take part. There are many more issues which might be significant in particular contexts, and to some extent the researchers will need to decide on what to explain having evaluated the specific features of the research.

Sometimes researchers will go as far as asking respondents to sign a document acknowledging that they have been informed about the research, and giving their formal agreement to take part. There is no reason why this should not be done, although in some contexts it may seem rather formal. **Ethical contracts** of this type may be rather reassuring for a research team, because they feel they will have received an absolute commitment from respondents. However, this may be rather disconcerting for some potential respondents, and there is always the possibility that they will withdraw from the research if confronted with the idea of signing a declaration of some kind.

Points to consider

Informed consent only has meaning as a concept if all potential respondents are genuinely 'informed'. A written summary of the research may be comprehensible to one respondent, but not to another. It may be necessary to explain the research in different ways to different people, in order to ensure that everyone is making a decision based upon full understanding.

Two of the major areas which are of concern to would-be respondents are **anonymity** and **confidentiality**. A researcher or research team will usually have a fairly good idea about the people who will have access to the research report when it is published. A journal article on a very specialist subject may be destined to be published in a small circulation journal, which will only be purchased by a relatively small number of specialized academics or researchers around the world. A short research paper may not actually be destined for publication, but might merely be circulated informally among professional friends. On the other hand, a chapter in an edited book may be destined for fairly large-scale publication, perhaps by a commercial publisher. In other words, research findings along with extracts of data may have, on the one hand, a rather minimal circulation to, on the other, a relatively major, commercial distribution. Respondents ought to be told the approximate limits of circulation of the final research report containing their data. In other words, they should be aware of the extent of the confidentiality of the research publication.

There is another aspect to confidentiality, and that is the issue of whether the data will be presented as coming from an individual, or whether the data will be combined or aggregated. If the latter, then it is usually much more difficult or even impossible to identify data which come from an individual. There are therefore consequences both for confidentiality and also for anonymity.

It tends to be a basic principle of social science research that as far as possible the anonymity of respondents will be preserved. There will be occasions when respondents will say that they are quite happy to be identified, either because they perhaps feel there are no major issues of concern, or because they might genuinely feel that it is in the wider public interest to know who was involved in the research. However, in such situations there is always the possibility that they might later on change their minds, or that others involved in the social situation may prefer that there is no identification of the context. Given the potential uncertainty for the future, many researchers feel that it is always preferable to maintain anonymity. There are several ways of preserving anonymity in the research report in a thesis.

One of the commonest methods is to give a fictional name to each respondent. If there are multiple respondents, a researcher will have to maintain a 'code list' in order to be able to remember which fictional name applies to a particular respondent. Clearly this list should be destroyed as soon as the research report is completed, in order to preserve anonymity. When selecting fictional names, researchers may also decide that it is desirable to employ names which reflect the gender, culture, ethnicity or religion of the original respondents. The other possibility to preserve anonymity is to give code numbers or letters to identify individuals. This, however, can seem rather formal and impersonal in a research report.

Of course whatever the precautions taken to preserve anonymity, there are a variety of issues which may prejudice it. These will usually involve the contextual information in a research report, such as information about the institution in which someone works. If it is recorded that someone was the principal of a college in a particular year, then it might be possible for the identity to be revealed if the name of the college were known. It therefore becomes important to be completely consistent with regard to anonymity, and to anonymize not only individuals but also places, institutions, and areas of a country. However, even in such a situation, a researcher may wish to cite documents about an institution for example, and these documents, if placed in the list of references, will then reveal the identity of that institution. In other words, once we embark on the task of maintaining anonymity, we need to be consistent with every aspect of the research which might indicate an identity.

 Questions to consider

As the research report or thesis is being written it is very important to ask oneself:

- Are there any clues in the text which might reveal the identity of respondents?
- Is it possible that other people might gain access to the report and hence breach my promises of confidentiality?

A general debate which permeates a great deal of ethical discussion generally, is that of the tension between what we might term **absolutist** and **relativist** ethics. If we assert that there are certain moral principles to which we should always adhere, no matter what the circumstances are, then we are, in a sense, advocating a form of absolutist ethics. For example, if we believe that it is always morally wrong to take the life of another human being then we would never participate in armed conflict, no matter what the justification might be or the threat to ourselves. On the other hand, relativist ethics as a principle points to the idea that moral dilemmas are extremely complex, and that it is often very difficult to decide what course of action is morally desirable. These two broad schools of thought clearly represent extremes at the ends of a continuum, and there are many intermediate positions which one might take.

These two broad approaches can be used as a means of analysis in research situations. For example, there is considerable debate around the issue of **covert** research. Let us take the example of a teacher-researcher collecting data in the school in which he or she teaches. In such situations, teachers will normally obtain the permission of the head teacher, and will also make it generally known, at least among some colleagues, that they are collecting data for a research study. In other words, they would try to be as open as possible about their intentions. However, situations may arise where they will be talking in a staff room and will decide to use some of what they hear as data. It may simply be too formal to interrupt the discussion and make a statement that some or all of what is said may be used as data. Equally, in such a situation, researchers may at the time have no particular intention to use the data in the study, but will merely note down what they hear out of background interest. Later on they may feel this is useful, and would wish to include it. Do they then go back to the people concerned and formally ask their permission? Real situations during data collection can often be relatively complex. However, if one were an absolutist about this issue of covert research, then one would always, no matter what the circumstances are, inform potential respondents and ask their permission. This would be done, no matter how apparently insignificant were the data. On the other hand, if one subscribed to a more relativist school of thought then researchers would probably make known their general intentions to colleagues, but would not feel constrained to inform people about every small piece of data collected. They would tend to use their judgement in individual cases.

It does seem that the very notion of covert, undisclosed research contravenes that important principle of informed consent. However, there are occasions when some researchers would argue that this could be justified. The usual type of justification provided is that, in order to collect data, a certain degree of covert activity will be involved, and secondly, that covert research is likely to be in the public good. These may or may not be persuasive arguments, depending upon one's point of view. For example, in a study of discrimination at work, if a manager employs practices which are discriminatory that manager would not normally freely disclose those procedures. In order to investigate the situation, covert research may be the only practical means available. The researchers may argue that by revealing the discriminatory practices, they are making life much fairer for a large number of people, and that this outweighs the general undesirability of covert research. There is probably no final way of resolving this issue, as much depends upon one's personal ethical world view. As examples of the debate here, Lugosi (2006) and Calvey (2008) both discuss the complexities of the issue of covert research.

The general argument in ethics that 'the end justifies the means' is supported by some people in certain circumstances. However, in evaluating such an issue, it may very much depend upon the 'ends' which we have in mind, and the 'means' which we intend to use to accomplish those ends. This is a form of relativist argument, and those who subscribe to an absolutist position on ethical questions would automatically reject certain means as absolutely undesirable. The general term for a moral argument which focuses upon the outcomes of moral decision making is 'consequentialism'. In other words, the decision making revolves around issues concerning the likely consequences of events. **Utilitarianism** is a particular form of consequentialism which argues that we should act in such a way that results in the greatest good for the largest number of people. Logically, this depends upon looking into the future, and it raises questions about whether it is possible to determine how many people will benefit from an action. There is also an issue about what is meant by 'good'. Trying to put the principle of utilitarianism into practice demands that we make a moral and practical judgement about the events which will benefit someone. Making this kind of decision inevitably involves applying one's own values, since ethical decision taking can never be **value free**.

One of the difficulties with utilitarianism, and focusing primarily upon the outcomes of a course of action, is that it may lead us gradually and inexorably towards actions which we suddenly realize are completely morally reprehensible. We become so obsessed with the results that we hope to acquire, that we forget about the morality of what we are doing.

? **Questions to consider**

In the process of social science research it is therefore important for researchers to ask themselves continually:

- Am I fully confident in the morality of how I am collecting these data?
- Am I sure that I am not taking advantage of respondents in any way?

We can avoid this danger to some extent by adopting a different approach known as **situation ethics**. As its name suggests, this approach tries to avoid all of the principles of moral action which restrict what we are willing to do, and argues instead that each moral situation is different and requires an individual analysis. In situation ethics then, there may be occasions when we would consider the consequences of actions, but there will also be occasions when we would focus upon the methods we are using. This is not to say that situation ethics does not possess moral principles, but that how we apply them, and indeed which principles we select for emphasis, depends upon the individual moral dilemmas which we face.

Critics of situation ethics, while no doubt impressed by the freedom given by the approach, would also no doubt be unimpressed by the apparent absence of guidelines for reaching a decision. Critics may say that situation ethics is in effect arguing that people can take whatever decision they like, as long as they feel they can justify it. To put it another way, they may feel that there is a lack of moral direction.

The act of providing ethical guidance can come from a variety of sources, and two terms sometimes used in this context are **beneficence** and **non-maleficence**. Beneficence is the general action of doing good for people, or of trying to improve their situation. In research terms, this might mean deliberately trying to find projects which are likely to benefit people in a significant manner; attempting to find ways in which the research project, or the providing of data, can specifically help the respondents; or perhaps using participation in a research project as a mechanism for teaching, so that participants actually do acquire knowledge while taking part in research.

The other principle is non-maleficence, which is arguably a rather more negative moral criterion. This asserts that we should act in such a way that we do not damage people or cause them any kind of undesirable outcome. For example, in interview research if the researcher started asking very personal questions then the respondent might begin to feel under stress. Carrying out the research in this way would be acting contrary to the principle of non-maleficence.

Practicalities of data collection

The issue of research ethics is often a very practical matter, concerned with research design and the ways in which we intend to go about collecting data. While as in the previous section, we may be concerned with general moral principles in our decision making, research ethics often becomes a question of resolving dilemmas in practical situations. One such question is the way in which we go about gaining **access** to the research field, and the way in which we request **permission** to conduct the research. These issues are interconnected, and thus raise interesting procedural and ethical questions.

First of all, it would be unfair to try to collect data in a particular situation without the authority or permission of those people who are responsible for that situation. In general terms if we were to try to collect data from within a school for example, without the knowledge and permission of the head teacher, then this might reasonably be regarded as at the very least unfair and inappropriate. A researcher might collect and disseminate data which the head teacher would prefer remained private. This argument, of course, does not take into account a situation where a very strong argument is made for covert research, on the grounds that something serious is taking place which it is in the public interest to know. It is normally assumed by social science researchers that they must obtain permission to conduct research from the person who has administrative authority for an organization, company, workplace, or physical location. This person is often termed a 'gatekeeper'.

When such permission is being requested researchers will often have to justify the nature and purpose of the research project. It may be necessary to furnish credentials for the research team, and to provide a list of those people who are requesting access to the site. This may be a requirement for insurance purposes. In addition, the researchers will probably need to justify the type of research to be carried out. This is a variant of the principle of informed consent, as it is only reasonable to provide such gatekeepers with the full information on which they can take a reasoned and informed decision.

As a separate issue, however, there is the question of how researchers will obtain ethical permission to conduct the research at all. In other words, how do they go about showing that their research design, aims, and data collection methods do not raise any serious issues of concern which might be perceived within the research community as making the research inappropriate?

Many organizations now have formally-constituted research ethics committees, which will meet regularly to consider approval requests for research projects. This is certainly true of universities and health or medical organizations. It is often a condition for institutional support for a research project that ethics approval or 'clearance' has been obtained. Those organizations – whether governmental, private or charitable – which provide research grants and funding, will usually also require some form of ethics approval before making grants. Ethics committees are acting to protect the interests of a number of different parties to the research. Firstly they are trying to protect respondents, so that they are not being asked to do anything which might cause them harm. Secondly they are trying to protect the researchers themselves, so that they do not inadvertently prejudice their professional reputations. And thirdly the committee is thinking about the institution which is sponsoring the research. The professional reputation of an institution may be harmed if it is seen as supporting inappropriate research studies.

Research ethics approval is particularly important where it is intended to collect data from people who are considered vulnerable in some way, or are in a context which is perceived as **sensitive**. Sensitive contexts may be understood as those where respondents may not be thought of as capable of giving rational responses. Research with respondents who have intellectual, perceptual, or cognitive difficulties would pose particular ethical dilemmas. It may, for example, be difficult to ensure that respondents are capable of giving their fully informed consent. Some respondents may be providing data in a language which is not their mother tongue, and this may be seen as posing ethical problems. Among the requirements for the research project to be seen as ethical, are that respondents have an acceptable degree of understanding of the nature and purpose of the research. Respondents should have a completely free choice over whether or not to participate in the research. They should not be subject to any undue persuasion or constraints, which will in any way limit their freedom of action or choice. In other words, if they agree to take part in the research, it should be as a fully autonomous individual capable of accepting or refusing the request.

Particular difficulties will arise where it is intended to collect data from school children. The latter are normally perceived as of insufficient maturity to be able to give informed consent totally on their own behalf, and hence permission must be obtained from others. It would be normal to consult at least the head teacher and other teachers who know the children, as well as the parents. In both practical and ethical terms, it would also be necessary to explain the anticipated research to the children and to indicate what would be expected of them. Even if they cannot understand all the subtleties of the research project, it is still important that the researchers try to explain it in an appropriate level of language.

Many different kinds of research are conducted with the help of school pupils, and the level of permission required may to some extent depend on the subject matter. For instance, a research project may seek to analyse the writing style and use of grammar when writing essays. This research might mean collecting essays written by pupils as part of their normal school work, and carrying out a form of linguistic analysis. The research might be used, in part, to assist the teachers in helping the children to improve their writing style. In other words, the 'research' could be viewed as simply the kind of activity that teachers would normally engage in if they had the time. On the other hand, research might involve trying to collect data on the social relationships of children both inside and outside school. It could be that to conduct the research, fairly detailed interviewing is envisaged. In such a case, where the research exceeds what would normally be done in a school environment, much more detailed and rigorous processes of obtain ethical approval would be required.

It is very difficult to be prescriptive about what kind of ethical approval and permission would be required in every case. As a general rule, however, this is not something which should be treated lightly, and every step should be taken to obtain permission from anyone considered significant in that research context. If it does not seem entirely clear who should be consulted, then probably the best strategy would be to consult as widely as practically possible, and to document carefully the process a researcher has gone through.

Many professional and educational organizations will try to document their recommended research ethics policy in a **code of practice**, and many of these are available for researchers to consult. Despite all that has been written on research ethics, the nature of ethical questions means that it is seldom, if ever, possible to give precise answers to ethical dilemmas, unless, of course, one is a strict moral absolutist. This is also evident in the field of research ethics. Most researchers are faced with the dilemma at some stage, of having done all that they think will be construed as reasonable in the situation, and of then continuing with their research. They may never feel absolutely confident that they have done everything they might do, but at some stage the decision has to be taken on whether or not to commence the research.

In some research projects, although not all by any means, it will be decided to **remunerate** respondents for taking part in the research. This may simply involve the reimbursement of travelling expenses, but if it involves actual payment for participation then it may raise ethical issues. A problem might arguably arise where an inducement, financial or otherwise, is offered to respondents which persuades them to participate, perhaps against their better judgement. This could be a particular matter of concern if the inducement were paid to people who are less affluent, and to whom the money might be a real attraction. More affluent people might be in a position to refuse to take part, as the money would be less necessary for them. On the other hand, one might argue that all respondents give of their time to provide data, and it is not at all unreasonable that they should be recompensed for this time they have given up. This once again is an ethical area which is rather vague, but it is at least an issue of which researchers should be conscious.

Social science research does make demands upon people, and notably upon those who agree to provide data. We all have some rights in terms of our personal **privacy**, and yet by its very nature, research seeks to encourage us to divulge either information or opinions which we might normally keep to ourselves. This simple feature of social research should never be treated as insignificant. Researchers should always remember that they are asking for something quite significant from respondents, and should always treat respondents accordingly.

 **Summary**

Researchers and organizations are becoming more and more aware of the issues of research ethics. It is perhaps part of a general trend in society that people are also becoming more and more aware of their rights in terms of what organizations do to us, or in our name. The subject of research ethics seeks to delineate the principles which should govern the conduct of researchers when collecting data, and the particular strategies which they should employ. This chapter has tried to examine some of the terms and concepts employed in this complex field.

 **Further reading**

Campbell, E. (2003) *The Ethical Teacher*. Maidenhead: Open University Press.
Farrell, A. (ed.) (2005) *Ethical Research with Children*. Maidenhead: Open University Press.
Hart, C. (2004) *Doing your Masters Dissertation*. London: SAGE.
Oliver, P. (2008) *Writing your Thesis* (2nd edn). London: SAGE.
Thomas, G. (2009) *How to Do your Research Project*. London: SAGE.

9

Presenting a Conclusion and Disseminating Research

 Chapter objectives

This chapter will help you to:

- Understand how to formulate and present the results of a research study.
- Develop your findings for publication in an academic journal.
- Find ways to disseminate your findings in professional reports.

Presenting the results of a research study

One of the criticisms sometimes levelled at social science and education research is that its findings are predictable and trite. They tend to express what the average person would expect to happen anyway. To take a fictional example, a research team might explore the effect on pupils' information technology skills of funding the purchase of a lot more school computers. The researchers might conclude that the extra computers appeared to result in enhanced computer skills. One can imagine parents asking why a lot of money was spent on a research project to tell them what seems to be obvious. While one can appreciate the scepticism about social science research, there are a few points which should be made here.

First of all, one of the purposes of research is to investigate the world systematically and to identify evidence for assertions, rather than simply believing what seems obvious. Sometimes the obvious is not as accurate as we may think. For example, in the case of the school computers, there could actually be other reasons for the improved ability in information technology. The pupils could be meeting regularly at the houses of friends, playing computer games, surfing the net, and hence improving their skills. The improvement could be part of what we might term a 'natural maturation process'. The school computers may well have helped, but might be only a part of a more complex process. As we have suggested on several occasions in this book, the relationship between variables is seldom a simple one-to-one relationship. It is usually more like a network, where there is a complex interplay of variables and causal factors.

It is very important then that when results are described we are circumspect in the way we present them. We may feel, for example, that the new school computers have been a very significant factor in pupil improvement in information technology, but we should express this in such a way that we leave open the possibility of other factors which we have not had the time to investigate. It is also perhaps worth reflecting upon the need to explain more about the limitations of research to members of the public. People would not then have rather high expectations of the extent to which research can provide dramatic new understandings of the world. A legitimate function of research, for example, is to seek to falsify some of our assumptions about the world. In trying to do this, we might in effect simply support what people have always assumed to be true. Nevertheless, we will now have evidence to support these popular assumptions rather than people having to rely upon what others will tell them.

? Questions to consider

Having written the conclusion to a research study it is important to re-read it with a critical eye, asking oneself:

- Have the results been qualified sufficiently?
- Have the limitations to the findings been sufficiently explained?
- Have the limitations of the research methodology been sufficiently analysed?

Researchers will sometimes use the popular media or newspapers to provide brief summaries of research, in order to draw public attention to their findings. It is important when presenting such findings to explain the limitations of the research. This may be particularly true with statistical research, where there may often be confusion about the limits of what statistics do, or do not, claim. Contrary to many of the assumptions of the general public, statistical findings do not represent certainty in any way. They provide an indication of the probability or otherwise, that a relationship between variables exists, or that we may anticipate something happening in the future. Once we accept this, then we can use the statistics simply as a guide.

It is very important as a principle to bring research findings into the public domain. While research remains a private activity, and the researcher does not submit his or her findings to others, then there is no possibility that the results can be falsified or provisionally verified. Once results are brought into the public domain, it is first of all a statement of confidence in the results by the researcher, and secondly, the creation of a situation by which someone else can examine the results objectively. One of the traditional ways in which this is achieved is through the research conference, devoted to research on a specific topic. This enables the community of academics and researchers interested in an area to share their research, and to invite others to replicate their work.

It must be acknowledged, however, that research in education and the social sciences is of very different kinds. Depending upon the methodology used, the findings may take very different forms. In ethnographic research, for example, the findings may take the form primarily of a descriptive account of an individual setting, a community, a school, or another establishment. The description will provide an account of the key actors in the setting, the different social relationships, and the actions of those who are part of this social world. Besides the description, however, there will be an attempt to reveal some of the relationships between the key individuals in the social setting, and also an attempt to understand some of the social forces which are operating. For example, there may be an attempt to understand the loci of power in an institution, which may not simply reside with the chief executive. There might be several different individuals or groups which exercise considerable influence over the social setting. There may also be an attempt to relate the organization to external society, in terms of revealing the range of relationships and professional links which exist. Besides simply describing the setting which is the subject of the ethnography, there will probably be an attempt to understand the organization, and to appreciate how its structure and functions are both the same as, and different from, those of similar organizations.

There are parallels here with the ways in which the conclusions of life history research may be presented. On one level, such findings may take the form literally of the life history of a person. Naturally such a life history will be selective, partly as a result of the data offered by the respondent, but also because of time constraints on the respondent. However, there is not necessarily a great deal which can be gleaned from a single life history per se. What is needed at this point is to relate that life to the general social and historical situation in which it has been forged, and to try to appreciate how the respondent has affected and influenced others. Moreover, it is also important that the particular life in question is compared and contrasted with the lives of other people who perhaps started off in a similar social class background, or even perhaps, by virtue of contrast, who came from a very different social milieu. It is this process of generalization which transforms the individual situation into something more significant, something which is important on a wider stage. With both of these examples of research, it is vital not to leave them at the level of the particular, but to draw out those issues which can make the research of note in a broader context.

The same is clearly true of case study research where the ultimate purpose is to relate an individual case to a wider social setting, and to illuminate its broader significance. In action research, the research findings or conclusions may be very different from the above examples. Action research was very much influenced by the philosophy of American pragmatism, and is concerned with the need to resolve practical issues in life, notably in the workplace. It is not an approach dedicated to the investigation of something simply because its resolution may be intrinsically interesting, or because the findings may prove useful in the future. The entire purpose of action research is to identify something which needs changing or improving, and to try to achieve this.

The other interesting aspect of action research is that it tends to involve both researchers and respondents in the research design process. In other words, it is not simply a group of professional researchers who will plan the project and in effect 'decide' what will happen to respondents. Rather research is seen as a collaborative effort, where everyone is involved in the resolution of a collective difficulty, perhaps at work or in the community. The research findings will then manifest themselves as an improved system, rather than as a theoretical report. This improved system will enable those involved in the research to do things in a more effective manner. However that is not the end of the research. Action research is often said to proceed in cycles, and the new system will now be subjected to tests to investigate whether it would be possible to improve its functioning. The research cycle would then operate once more.

There are other forms of research which also aspire to resolve practical problems, but the aim may be rather more implicit than explicit. For example, interactionist research may be used to explore the relationships between people in an organization, perhaps a school, college or hospital, with the result that human systems are altered to improve the working environment. The research may have other aims – for example, to investigate the effects of a particular management style. Nevertheless, the practical outcomes may be, to all intents and purposes, rather similar to the results of an action research study.

While discussing the practical uses of research, it is worth mentioning some of the developments in the way doctoral research is being presented. In recent years a number of alternatives to the traditional, single thesis of the Doctor of Philosophy (PhD) have been developed. The main development has been in the creation of the so-called 'professional' doctorates which are usually associated with a specific discipline. The best-known example is perhaps the Doctor of Education (EdD) but analogous qualifications exist in a range of disciplines, including nursing and other health-related professions and management and business studies. Such doctoral programmes usually involve a taught element associated with the particular profession, and a shorter thesis than with a PhD. In some programmes there is more than one short thesis in order to allow the student to develop a number of research ideas, albeit in less depth than would be the case with a traditional doctorate. The rationale for such doctorates is that they are more closely aligned with a particular profession, and hence more effective as a preparation for senior professional roles than the PhD. It may be that there is rather more of a tendency for the students on professional doctorates to select topics for their theses which have a more professional or vocational orientation that is the case with the PhD, although this is perhaps awaiting a thorough investigation.

Certainly the professional doctorate thesis is considered as a research thesis, in the same way as a PhD, and evaluated according to the same criteria. Nevertheless, there remains the perception that the professional doctorate is arguably more vocationally and professionally oriented in terms of its purposes. This does leave a situation of some ambiguity, where the aims of the two types of programme are not quite as distinct, or as clearly delineated, as might be the case. It could be argued, for example, that the PhD is intended to prepare the individual for an academic career, while the professional doctorate is intended to prepare someone for the career of a senior professional who also happens to be a scholar. However, once again further research would be needed to establish whether subsequent career pathways could correlate with this perhaps rather simplistic distinction. There is a developing literature on the subject of professional doctorates. Galvin and Carr (2003) examined the nature of professional doctorates in nursing and analysed the views of staff and students, while Shulman et al. (2006) analysed the apparent differences between the PhD and professional doctorates in Education.

Points to consider

It is worth remembering that much of the research which is carried out initially simply to investigate an issue out of interest may later develop practical uses. Understanding the social world around us is often the first step to our taking action to improve it.

Some types of research methodology will have an avowedly political perspective, in that in carrying out a research project the researchers hope to have such a significant effect upon the balance of power in society, or to change the way groups in society are perceived. This is particularly evident in the case of feminist research, where many projects hope not only to draw attention to inequalities in society, and normally situations where women are placed in a position of disadvantage, but moreover, to try to transform such situations. Research conducted within the parameters of Marxist theory will also be political, in the sense that a Marxist perspective will seek first of all to analyse situations in society where there are significant economic differences, but will then try to change those economic differences. Such research may, in a classical Marxist sense, try to analyse society within a framework of those who control capital, and those who are employed to try to earn capital for others.

Some Marxist-inspired research has also attempted to show that the educational system in effect reproduces the cultural conditions which enable one stratum of society to perpetuate their wealth and privilege, at the expense of a different stratum (often a considerably larger one) who have access only to a less-advantageous educational system for their children. Again, such research attempts to transform these inequalities and hence is political in nature.

Some social science research presents its conclusions almost as a 'story'. This is true of life history research, autobiographical studies, stream of consciousness accounts, and oral narratives. The data here may not be very different to some books which one might find in a public library. There are also some perhaps experimental forms of social science research, where a researcher will write a fictional account which attempts to reflect some of the research findings using more orthodox methods. Such fictional accounts, perhaps reflecting a type of phenomenological approach, are designed to explore a different medium within which to describe the world.

Finally, there are forms of research in which someone working in a particular location or profession will conduct research in the very milieu in which they work. The 'teacher-researcher' is a case in point, but the approach could also be applied to nurses or doctors, for example, researching some aspects of the setting in which they work. The findings from such studies are very often work-focused and designed to analyse or explore particular facets of the work environment.

Publishing findings in an academic journal

The academic journal is the principal medium for the dissemination of research findings in any subject. All of the main subject areas of research, and many of the areas of minority interest, have academic journals devoted to them. Journals exist in many different languages and are increasingly available on the internet.

It is clearly important that research findings published in academic journals are as trustworthy as possible. One of the ways in which both the general quality of the articles – and also of the findings – are assured, is through the process of peer review. Most academic journals will carry the statement somewhere that they are 'peer reviewed'. Upon receipt of an article, an editor will usually send copies to at least two reviewers who will be academics from the particular field covered by the article. The author's name will be deleted to encourage an independent, objective review and to maintain their anonymity. Reviewers will then be asked to indicate the strengths and weaknesses of the article, and to recommend (or otherwise) that it be published. Editors may reserve the right to consult a third party if the first two reviewers prove not to be in agreement.

One problem with the journal article as a means of dissemination is that there can be a considerable time lapse between the submission and acceptance of an article and its final publication. In order to improve this situation many academic journals are now available on-line, which reduces the waiting time considerably. Also, in the case of some research subjects, it is important that findings are placed in the public domain as soon as possible.

Points to consider

Some academic journals provide a note of the key dates in the history of the acceptance of an article. For example, they might note the date of submission and the date of acceptance. These dates give an indication to potential authors of the typical speed of publication.

The peer review process does not necessarily guarantee the quality of all journal articles. Reviewers will differ in the weight they attach to different aspects of academic writing. In addition, it is not part of the review process to replicate the actual research. Reviewers can only form a judgement about the account of the research provided, and not the actual research. Nevertheless, if insufficient information is provided about, say, the methodology, then this might be an indication of the thoroughness of the process. The peer review process may not be perfect, but it is perhaps the best system which can be operated given the very large number of articles which are written and submitted each year. Moreover, the review process becomes very important in another sense, given the importance which research publications increasingly have for academics and researchers. The career progression of the latter is often judged at least partly by considering the number of research publications they have achieved. It is important, therefore, that this process is as fair, objective, balanced, and efficient as possible.

The management of an academic journal will usually be carried out by an editor, assistant editor, and a group of academics who are specialists in the subject area of the journal. Most or all of these individuals will normally be practising or perhaps recently-retired academics. They perform this duty out of an interest and commitment to their subject, and also because there is a certain prestige in being attached to a well-known academic journal. The editor will take the advice of the individuals who have reviewed a particular article, but will retain the power to make the final decision or to refer the article to another reviewer.

When reading an academic journal article there are a number of factors to bear in mind. First of all, the length of an article will impose a number of restrictions upon its author. A typical article may be of about 8000 words, which is a tenth of the length of a PhD thesis for example. Nevertheless, and despite its relative brevity, this article may describe a substantial piece of research. Inevitably then, some elements of the account may be rather foreshortened. The review of relevant literature may only allude to certain key works or previous research, and the account of the research design may only be able to summarize aspects of the methodology, omitting some of the theoretical discussion which might be included in a longer account. It is also the case that researchers will sometimes subdivide a longer piece of research, and report it in several different articles over a period of time, or even to be published in different journals. In such a case, each article will only present a snapshot of the particular aspect of the research project being described.

Disseminating findings in professional reports

There are many other vehicles for publishing research findings than academic journals, although the latter are probably seen as the most prestigious. To start perhaps with the most populist, radio and the quality press will often carry journalistic reports of research, usually because they are perceived as having a news value or being in the public interest. Researchers are often happy for this kind of publicity, because it draws public attention to the work they are doing and also perhaps to the public importance of their work. Almost certainly, however, their research will have been previously written up and published in more orthodox academic contexts.

There are also popular and professional journals which, while being serious publications, will at the same time probably contain photographs and illustrations that will mark them out as being rather more populist that academic journals, and which will rarely carry illustrations other than graphical representations, table of figures, or statistical data. Such professional journals are often very happy to carry brief reports of research which are relevant to their professional area. These add credibility to the journal and keep readers informed of the latest developments.

Other forms of dissemination include situations where the researcher provides a talk or presentation on the research. The most formal of these is the research conference, which is sometimes organized in conjunction with, or under the auspices of, an academic journal. The researcher submits a 'paper' for consideration by the conference committee. The paper is a brief summary of the research, often rather like a shortened version of an academic article, although actual practice will differ from conference to conference. Copies of the paper are made available to attendees, and all of the papers from the conference are often published as 'conference proceedings'. There will also sometimes be opportunities for on-going research to be reported not as a formal presentation but perhaps as a poster presentation, which conference attendees can read and then later perhaps discuss with the researcher.

Finally, it should not be forgotten that research is also published in book form. Some publishers specialize in the publication of relatively small circulation books, which are based largely upon recent empirical research. This form of dissemination has all the advantages that come from publication as a book, but the disadvantages encompass the relatively long time required by the publication process, and the relatively small circulation, often largely restricted to academic libraries.

Summary

The dissemination of research is fundamental to its credibility and to its capacity to influence society. Research findings should always be subject to replication by others in order to give confidence in the research process, and in the open nature of the way in which researchers work. Equally, research findings need to be brought into the public domain, not merely to facilitate their potential verification, but also to enable other professionals or members of the public to act on them where appropriate.

Further reading

Blakeslee, A.M. and Fleischer, C. (2007) *Becoming a Writing Researcher.* Abingdon: Routledge.

Lunenburg, F.C. and Irby, B.J. (2008) *Writing a Successful Thesis or Dissertation.* London: Corwin.

O'Leary, Z. (2004) *The Essential Guide to Doing Research.* London: SAGE.

Thomas, R.M. and Brubaker, D.L. (2007) *Theses and Dissertations: A Guide to Planning, Research and Writing* (2nd edn). London: Corwin.

Wallace, M. and Wray, A. (2006) *Critical Reading and Writing for Postgraduates.* London: SAGE.

References

Allan, H.T. (2006) 'Using participant observation to immerse oneself in the field', *Journal of Research in Nursing*, 11 (5): 397–407.

Anagnostou, Y. (2009) 'A critique of symbolic ethnicity: the ideology of choice?', *Ethnicities*, 9 (1): 94–140.

Apple, M.W. (2008) 'Can schooling contribute to a more just society?', *Education, Citizenship and Social Justice*, 3 (3): 239–261.

Bahre, E. (2007) 'Reluctant solidarity: death, urban poverty and neighbourly assistance in South Africa', *Ethnography*, 8 (1): 33–59.

Berger, P.L. and Luckmann, T. (1967) *The Social Construction of Reality*. Harmondsworth: Penguin.

Bowen, D. (2002) 'Research through participant observation in Tourism: a creative solution to the measurement of consumer satisfaction/dissatisfaction (CS/D) among tourists', *Journal of Travel Research*, 41 (1): 4–14.

Boyd, D. et al. (2008) 'Surveying the landscape of teacher education in New York City: constrained variation and the challenge of innovation', *Educational Evaluation and Policy Analysis*, 30 (4): 319–343.

Bryman, A. (2006) 'Integrating quantitative and qualitative research: how is it done?', *Qualitative Research*, 6 (1): 97–113.

Bulterman-Bos, J.A. (2008) 'Will a clinical approach make educational research more relevant for practice?', *Educational Researcher*, 37 (7): 412–420.

Cain, D.J. (2003) 'Advancing humanistic psychology and psychotherapy: some challenges and proposed solutions', *Journal of Humanistic Psychology*, 43 (3): 10–41.

Calloni, M. (ed.) (2003) 'Feminism, politics, theories and science: which new link?', *The European Journal of Women's Studies*, 10 (1): 87–103.

Calvey, D. (2008) 'The art and politics of covert research', *Sociology*, 42 (5): 905–918.

Carolan, M.S. (2008) 'The bright- and blind-spots of science: why objective knowledge is not enough to resolve environmental controversies', *Critical Sociology*, 34 (5): 725–740.

Chandra, K. and Wilkinson, S. (2008) 'Measuring the effect of "ethnicity"', *Comparative Political Studies*, 41 (4/5): 515–563.

Chiapello, E. (2003) 'Reconciling the two principal meanings of the notion of ideology: the example of the concept of the "spirit of capitalism"', *European Journal of Social Theory*, 6 (2): 155–171.

Clough, P. and Nutbrown, C. (2002) *A Student's Guide to Methodology*. London: SAGE.

Cook, T.D. (2002) 'Randomized experiments in educational policy research: a critical examination of the reasons the educational evaluation community has offered for not doing them', *Educational Evaluation and Policy Analysis*, 24 (3): 175–199.

Cook, T.D. (2003) 'Why have educational evaluators chosen not to do randomized experiments?', *The Annals*, 589 (1): 114–149.

Crandall, C.S. and Schaller, M. (2001) 'Social psychology and the pragmatic conduct of science', *Theory and Psychology*, 11 (4): 479–488.

Darbyshire, P., Macdougall, C. and Schiller, W. (2005) 'Multiple methods in qualitative research with children: more insight or just more?', *Qualitative Research*, 5 (4): 417–436.

Delorme, D.E., Kreshel, P.J. and Reid, L.N. (2003) 'Lighting up: young adults' autobiographical accounts of their first smoking experiences', *Youth and Society*, 34 (4): 468–496.

Diaz-Laplante, J. (2007) 'Humanistic psychology and social transformation: building the path toward a livable today and a just tomorrow', *Journal of Humanistic Psychology*, 47 (1): 54–72.

Dobles, I. (1999) 'Marxism, ideology and psychology', *Theory and Psychology*, 9 (3): 407–410.

Duckett, P., Sixsmith, J. and Kagan, C. (2008) 'Researching pupil well-being in UK secondary schools', *Childhood*, 15 (1): 89–106.

Enslin, P. (2003) 'Liberal feminism, diversity and education', *Theory and Research in Education*, 1 (1): 73–87.

Eskelinen, L. and Caswell, D. (2006) 'Comparison of social work practice in teams using a video vignette technique in a multi-method design', *Qualitative Social Work*, 5 (4): 489–503.

Ezeh, P-J., (2003) 'Participant observation', *Qualitative Research*, 3 (2): 191–205.

Farrington, D.P. (2003) 'A short history of randomized experiments in criminology', *Evaluation Review*, 27 (3): 218–227.

Fjellström, M. (2008) 'A learner-focused evaluation strategy: developing medical education through a deliberative dialogue with stakeholders', *Evaluation*, 14 (1): 91–106.

Furman, R., Langer, C.L., Davis, C.S., Gallardo, H.P. and Kulkarni, S. (2007) 'Expressive, research and reflective poetry as qualitative inquiry: a study of adolescent identity', *Qualitative Research*, 7 (3): 301–315.

Fook, J. (2002) 'Theorizing from practice: towards an inclusive approach for social work research', *Qualitative Social Work*, 1 (1): 79–95.

Galvin, K. and Carr, E. (2003) 'The emergence of professional doctorates in nursing in the UK: where are we now?', *Journal of Research in Nursing*, 8 (4): 293–307.

Gambaudo, S.A. (2007) 'French Feminism *vs* Anglo-American Feminism: a reconstruction', *European Journal of Women's Studies*, 14 (2): 93–108.

Garland, D. (2006) 'Concepts of culture in the sociology of punishment', *Theoretical Criminology*, 10 (4): 419–447.

Gerber, A.S. (2004) 'Does campaign spending work? Field experiments provide evidence and suggest new theory', *American Behavioral Scientist*, 47 (5): 541–574.

Giorgi, A. (2005) 'Remaining challenges for humanistic psychology', *Journal of Humanistic Psychology*, 45 (2): 204–216.

Green, D.P. and Gerber, A.S. (2003) 'The underprovision of experiments in political science', *The Annals*, 589 (1): 94–112.

Harnois, C.E. (2005) 'Different paths to different feminisms? Bridging multiracial feminist theory and quantitative sociological gender research', *Gender and Society*, 19 (6): 809–828.

Hayes, B.C. et al. (2000) 'Gender, postmaterialism, and feminism in comparative perspective', *International Political Science Review*, 21 (4): 425–439.

Hill, D.B. (2006) 'Theory in applied social psychology', *Theory and Psychology*, 16 (5): 613–640.

Joy, M. (2005) 'Humanistic psychology and animal rights: reconsidering the boundaries of the humanistic ethic', *Journal of Humanistic Psychology*, 45 (1): 106–130.

Kuhn, T.S. (1996) *The Structure of Scientific Revolutions* (3rd edn). Chicago: University of Chicago Press.

Leskelä-Kärki, M. (2008) 'Narrating life stories in between the fictional and the autobiographical', *Qualitative Research*, 8 (3): 325–332.

Lillis, T. (2008) 'Ethnography as method, methodology, and 'deep theorizing': closing the gap between text and context in academic writing research', *Written Communication*, 25 (3): 353–388.

Lugosi, P. (2006) 'Between overt and covert research', *Qualitative Inquiry*, 12 (3): 541–561.

Mahtani, M. (2002) 'What's in a name? Exploring the employment of 'mixed race' as an identification', *Ethnicities*, 2 (4): 469–490.

Maner, J.K. et al. (2007) 'Power, risk and the status quo: does power promote riskier or more conservative decision making?', *Personality and Social Psychology Bulletin,* 33 (4): 451–462.

Manning, P.K. (2001) 'Theorizing policing: the drama and myth of crime control in the NYPD', *Theoretical Criminology*, 5 (3): 315–344.

Markowitz, F. (2004) 'Talking about culture: globalization, human rights and anthropology', *Anthropological Theory*, 4 (3): 329–352.

Mason, J. (2002) *Qualitative Researching*. London: SAGE.

May, V. (2008) 'On being a 'good' mother: the moral presentation of self in written life stories', *Sociology*, 42 (3): 470–486.

McMurray, A.J. (2006) 'Teaching action research: the role of demographics', *Active Learning in Higher Education*, 7 (1): 37–50.

McNamara, P. (2009) 'Feminist ethnography: storytelling that makes a difference', *Qualitative Social Work*, 8 (2): 161–177.

McQuillan, P.J. (2005) 'Possibilities and pitfalls: a comparative analysis of student empowerment', *American Educational Research Journal*, 42 (4): 639–670.

Moore, K.S. (2008) 'Class formations: Competing forms of black middle-class identity', *Ethnicities*, 8(4): 492–517.

Nemeroff, T. (2008) 'Generating the power for development through sustained dialogue: an experience from rural South Africa', *Action Research*, 6 (2): 213–232.

Nickerson, D.W. (2006) 'Volunteer phone calls can increase turnout: evidence from eight field experiments', *American Politics Research*, 34 (3): 271–292.

Pager, D. (2007) 'The use of field experiments for studies of employment discrimination: contributions, critiques, and directions for the future', *The Annals*, 609 (1): 104–133.

Rae, A.M. and Cochrane, D.K. (2008) 'Listening to students: how to make written assessment feedback useful', *Learning in Higher Education*, 9 (3): 217–230.

Rigakos, G.S. and Law, A. (2009) 'Risk, realism and the politics of resistance', *Critical Sociology*, 35 (1): 79–103.

Rolfe, E. (2008) 'Refugee, minority, citizen, threat: Tibetans and the Indian refugee script', *South Asia Research*, 28 (3): 253–283.

Sa'ar, A. (2005) 'Postcolonial feminism, the politics of identification, and the Liberal bargain', *Gender and Society,* 19 (5): 680–700.

Savage, J. (2006) 'Ethnographic evidence: the value of applied ethnography in healthcare', *Journal of Research in Nursing*, 11 (5): 383–393.

Schiele, J.H. (2005) 'Cultural oppression and the high-risk status of African Americans', *Journal of Black Studies*, 35 (6): 802–826.

Shah, H. and Nah, S. (2004) 'Long ago and far away: how US newspapers construct racial oppression', *Journalism*, 5 (3): 259–278.

Shulman, L.S., Golde, C.M., Bueschel, A.C. and Garabedian, K.J. (2006) 'Reclaiming education's doctorates: a critique and a proposal', *Educational Researcher*, 35 (3): 25–32.

Smart, A. et al. (2008) 'The standardization of race and ethnicity in biomedical science editorials and UK biobanks', *Social Studies of Science*, 38 (3): 407–423.

Somech, A. (2005) 'Teachers' personal and team empowerment and their relations to organizational outcomes: contradictory or compatible constructs?', *Educational Administration Quarterly*, 41 (2): 237–266.

Stam, H.J. (2006) 'Introduction: reclaiming the *social* in social psychology', *Theory and Psychology*, 16 (5): 587–595.

Sundstrom, R.R. (2002) 'Race as a human kind', *Philosophy and Social Criticism*, 28 (1): 91–115.

Tate, W.F. (2008) '"Geography of opportunity": poverty, place and educational outcomes', *Educational Researcher*, 37 (7): 397–411.

Tonnelat, S. (2008) '"Out of frame": The (in)visible life of urban interstices – a case study in Charenton-le-Pont, Paris, France', *Ethnography*, 9 (3): 291–324.

Van Dijke, M. and Poppe, M. (2007) 'Motivations underlying power dynamics in hierarchically structured groups', *Small Group Research*, 38 (6): 643–669.

Vaughan, D. (2004) 'Theorizing disaster: analogy, historical ethnography, and the Challenger accident', *Ethnography*, 5 (3): 315–347.

Veltri, B.T. (2008) 'Teaching or service? The site-based realities of Teach for America teachers in poor, urban schools', *Education and Urban Society*, 40 (5): 511–542.

Voils, C.I., Sandelowski, M., Barroso, J. and Hasselblad, V. (2008) 'Making sense of qualitative and quantitative findings in mixed research synthesis studies', *Field Methods*, 20 (1): 3–25.

Vrasti, W. (2008) 'The strange case of ethnography and international relations', *Millennium: Journal of International Studies*, 37 (2): 279–301.

Walliman, N. (2006) *Social Research Methods*. London: SAGE.

Index